SUCCESSFUL FRANCHISING

The Fast Track To Profitability.

By

BRADLEY J. SUGARS

With
Grant McDuling

ISBN 0 9580932 9 6
FIRST EDITION

Published by *Action* International Pty Ltd
GPO Box 1340 Brisbane, QLD 4001
Phone: +61 (0) 7 3368 2525
Fax: +61 (0) 7 3368 2535
www.action-international.com

Distributed by *Action* International, for further information
contact +61 (0) 7 3368 2525

Printed in Australia by Pure Print

"Franchising is an exciting option that allows you to sell your business, over and over again, without losing control of the business. It is an option you could consider if you want to raise a large amount of money quickly."

Brad Sugars

Acknowledgements

Thanks to Rich Roberts, Communications Director of the Cendant Hotel Group, and to Howard Johnson International, Inc for details of the Howard Johnson story. And to Rani Schwager of *Action* United Kingdom for proof reading the draft.

■ CONTENTS

Introduction 1

The *Action* Story: Turning Dreams Into Reality 7

Humble Beginnings - The Birth Of A New Way Of Doing Business .. 25

So You Want To Buy A Franchise, Do You? 47

The Business Mindset 61

Buying A Franchise 81

Selling A Franchise 93

Franchising Your Business 111

Franchising - A Question Of Relationships 127

Conclusion 153

Getting Into *Action* 155

▌ Introduction

Did you know? ... _____

The Subway restaurant chain has been named the number one franchise opportunity for 2003 by Entrepreneurs Magazine in its 24th annual Franchise 500 rankings.

This was the 11th time in the past 15 years that this prestigious honour has been awarded to Subway.

Subway Restaurants is the world's largest submarine sandwich franchise, with more than 17,500 locations in 71 countries.

Headquartered in Milford, Connecticut, Subway was co-founded by Fred DeLuca and Peter Buck in 1965.

It's been said that there are many ways to fame and fortune, but as far as I can see, some are better than others. You could, for instance, become wealthy by winning the lotto, but who in their right mind would include this as a cornerstone of their financial strategy?

You could make your fortune through sport, but here again, you'd have to be very, very good at it to have any chance of realising your financial ambition. And you'd better ensure your chosen sport is one in which big pay cheques are par for the course. Try even covering your costs by taking part in judo or hockey!

You could marry into money. This has been done more than a few times. Or you could sing for your supper. All you need is one top ten song and you're laughing. Those that have the talent – and it is a talent – can make an extraordinary amount of money. The music industry is bulging with billionaires.

The trouble with these strategies is that they rely either on luck or a natural talent. But what if you aren't prepared to take the ultimate gamble? What if you weren't born with a natural sporting talent or a beautiful voice? What if you didn't have the creative juices to pen a catchy melody?

Well, there's always business.

That's right, business is, in my view, the surest way to wealth and riches. Once you've come to realise that being an employee will get you nowhere, you'll quickly understand what being in business can do for you. But you have to take that first step. You have to understand that, with few exceptions, the word JOB actually means **J**ust **O**ver **B**roke. And that's why I believe there are only two reasons for having a job: to gain knowledge and to accumulate capital. That's all. If you aren't learning anything new in your current job, or if you aren't accumulating capital to get started in business for yourself, then leave that job. It's that simple.

Hang on, I hear you say. What about investing in shares or real estate? Isn't that a way to look after your financial aspirations?

Sure they are, but in my view, they are best left until AFTER you've begun making sufficient returns through business. You see, by first accumulating profit from your business and then investing that in real estate or the stock market (and preferably in that order) you'll be ensuring you don't end up like so may 'financially secure' people – asset rich but cash poor! What's the point of that? Get the cash first, and then you can buy all the real estate or shares that you want.

So how do you get into business? Well, there are three proven routes.

- Firstly, you could start one yourself. This is probably the first choice of most people who want to go it alone. But is it the best? In business today, buying customers is the most expensive purchase you'll ever make. You're paying retail when you're buying customers. Let me explain this. If you spend $1,000 in advertising and get ten new customers, then you're paying $100 ($1,000/10) per new customer. Ask anyone who started a new company what the hardest part was, and by far and away, all will agree it was getting customers. Starting a business from scratch is also a huge waste of your most valuable asset – time. Think about it for a moment. Start your own business and it will take you somewhere between one and five years to become profitable. Buy an existing business that's already profitable (or just about profitable) and you've saved yourself those years. This is one very important lesson most people wish they had learnt when they first started out. Someone once said to me that the biggest reason people fail in business is a lack of start-up capital … yes that's true, but only because they started the business themselves and had to pay retail for everything.

- The second way of getting into business is to buy one wholesale. This is generally the method I recommend. So what exactly is buying wholesale? What does it mean? Essentially what we're looking at is a whole new frame of reference about buying stuff. Most people negotiate based on the advertised price. I negotiate based on the initial price of ZERO. That's right; most people work their way down from the advertised price, whereas I negotiate from zero and have them justify why it's worth anything at all. Sure, it takes a special kind of thinking to succeed in buying businesses this way. I live by a simple negotiation mantra … "I have more persistence than you have resistance". You see, I'm willing to wait and wait and wait until a deal works, and if the deal never works, then so be it … My golden rule is this: fall in love with the deal, not the business. One question that commonly arises when I start to mention buying a business for little or no money is; "Why would they sell it to me for so little?" Hopefully, you've already thought of a few answers. Most of the answers are emotional rather than logical: divorce, sickness, tiredness, pregnancy, travel, or just plain sick and tired of working too many hours for too little money. One final point: Buying wholesale takes discipline, it takes following up and abiding strictly by your investment rules. Anyone can go out and pay full price for a business. It takes an artist, an entrepreneur, to make a deal and have everyone leave the table happy.

- The third way of getting into business is to buy retail. What does this mean? To me you're paying retail if you buy the business for a price anywhere near the advertised price. And by anywhere near, I mean anything more than half of what they've advertised it for.

With this in mind there are several reasons why I recommend you should use this purchasing method.

However, I suggest that you only ever pay retail for your first few businesses. Firstly you need to get these first few running at a profit without you having to work in them. Then when you've got enough time and money, move on to wholesale deals. So, what are my reasons for paying the retail price? There are three:

Reason 1 ... At least you've got a start. The business is up and running, and making a profit. This profit is extremely important if you're paying retail. You want built-in profits that give you a planned return on investment before you even have to build the business. And, if you're paying full price, you want full profits. Make sure you get the previous owner to work with you for up to a month, as part of the purchase price, to train you. One important thing about the previous owner though is that they're still blinded by what you can't do, based on their experience. Always be willing to try something new, even though they may feel it won't work.

Reason 2 ... You're about to learn a lot. Whilst I'd recommend negotiating on the price, remember the main objective of your first business is to learn and grow, and secondly to make money and profits.

Reason 3 ... The most powerful time to pay retail is when you're investing in a proven Franchise. Franchising has removed many of the pitfalls for the business buyer. And whilst many franchise systems are great, there are also many that are pitiful. Many people starting franchises do so with no idea of how to support you or how to help you to succeed. Be aware the best franchises are generally the ones you will have to pay a solid price for. However, remember to look for profit, not turnover. One last point about buying at a retail price; whilst it's not the best way to buy, it's still a solid way for first-time buyers to invest in a proven system that can fast track both your profits and your learning experience.

This book is all about how to succeed in franchising. It's not about the different types of franchises that exist in the modern business world and it isn't intended to be an academic overview of this form of business. This book is all about helping YOU to navigate through the tides of franchising so you can make informed decisions about whether it is a viable option, what to ensure if you are selling a franchise, and what lies ahead if you are contemplating franchising an existing business.

This book is all about how to SUCCEED in franchising.

This book is about *Action*. It is based on real experiences and real examples. It contains powerful information that you can put to use RIGHT NOW.

And perhaps more importantly, this book is simple to understand. It is based on knowledge that I have acquired over the years. And it's tested knowledge - knowledge I have used myself for great personal reward.

This knowledge has been distilled so it's easy to understand and use straight away. So please, consider this book your personal coach. I will be imparting INVALUABLE knowledge about how to get on the fast track to profitability through franchising.

The *Action* Story: Turning Dreams Into Reality

Did you know? ...

Action International is the world's first business-to-business sales and marketing coaching firm.

When *Action* opened its doors for business, it was operated out of the back room of a suburban home in Brisbane, Australia.

Today *Action* operates out of more than 500+ offices throughout Australia, New Zealand, Asia, Canada, Mexico, Europe, the UK and the USA.

At this point, you might be asking yourself what qualifies me to write a book about how to succeed in franchising. And that's a fair question.

Let me tell you.

I believe I know a few things about succeeding in this industry because I've learnt the hard way. I've built my company, *Action* International, up from nothing to being ranked as the 19th Fastest Growing Franchise in the world, and ranked 123rd in the Top 500 by the USA's Entrepreneur magazine. And this has been achieved in just eight years!

Sure I've made mistakes along the way – after all, that's what learning is all about. But there's another important qualification I have for writing this book. I have studied how to succeed in franchising, because my business is all about coaching other businesses to succeed at what they do. You could say I have a vested interest in success.

And the systems I developed have successfully taken many businesses down the franchise path.

My story isn't unique – many others have realised their dreams just as I have. But it does go to show that you can achieve whatever you want if you're focused and committed. You need to have a vision, and you need to think big. Then you need to get into action. And it doesn't really matter how young or old you are. I started my first business when I was 15 and Colonel Harland Sanders of KFC fame was 65 when he used his $105 Social Security cheque to start his business.

My story is all about turning dreams into reality. And not just my dreams, but also the dreams of the countless thousands of business owners my coaches and I have worked with over the years.

My Dad decided I was going to be a businessman when he found me selling my Christmas presents to my brothers when I was only seven. The following year I'd become much smarter and worked out that if I just rented my toys to them for a day or two at a time, I got the money and the toys back afterwards.

I'm so glad now that I was a different kind of child, one who was so interested in business and money rather than just getting a job.

There is another thing that others may think of as a sin, but I now see as a virtue. I am UNEMPLOYABLE … I found this out when I was 15 and tried to have a part-time job, not realising that thinking for myself and outshining my boss wouldn't do me any favours.

It's been a long road since then, owning many businesses of all shapes and sizes, being awarded an accounting degree, making a lot of money, losing a lot of money, investing a lot of money, travelling the globe several times over, teaching hundreds of thousands of business people, writing several best-selling books and building a world-wide conglomerate. Also, living a great life with amazing relationships with my family, friends and business colleagues.

It all began, I guess, when, as a 15 year-old boy, I employed my friends as paper delivery boys and gleaned a few dollars for the papers they delivered. Since then my businesses have become a little more sophisticated, yet still based on the same principle. Which is finding something people want to buy, and selling it to them, making sure I charged well and gave great service.

By the time I'd finished University, I had completed a Bachelor of Business in Accounting and worked in 27 different jobs; ranging from gardener to pipe maker, from pizza cook to radio announcer, and from disc jockey to accounts clerk. And do you want to know the one thing this experience had taught me? It was this: very few people ever gave anything their best.

As soon as I'd left Uni, I got a sales job and invested every single dollar I earned into training myself. Courses on money, investing, sales, business, personal growth - you name it, I did a course in it. You see, I knew that to achieve what I wanted out of life wasn't going to be about how hard I worked, but about how much I knew.

By the time I was 21, I was running four retail stores and had a photocopy management contract, earning a salary of $60,000 a year.

My mum almost had a heart attack when I told her that I had quit to go and work for myself. Being young and naive was probably a good thing. I had no capital, but a lot of smart ideas on how to create sales, how to market and how to lead a team of people.

I bought into a ladies fashion store with no money down. What I offered them instead of money for my 33% holding was the ability to create sales.

You reckon that was foolish of them, don't you? Well, I increased sales by 93% over the first nine weeks and sold my interest back to the other partners just three months later.

I did the same with a pizza manufacturing business; I took their product from just being sold in cafes to having it stocked on the shelves of Woolworths, as well as almost every other small retailer in Queensland. I funded this growth with my earnings from the ladies wear store.

I was, at the same time, doing some business consulting during my spare time.

It was this consulting work that really led me to where I am today. One gentleman I offered my services to *(I used to give away two hours of my time for free, just so people could understand what I could do for them)* operated an international training company. This gentleman was best selling author Robert Kiyosaki. He asked me to come and train his seminar promoters in the art of marketing. Little did I know then what was in store.

Training 30 seminar promoters in Hawaii meant that I was bound to go into the presenting business. Seminars in Hong Kong, New Zealand and in Melbourne meant the sale of the pizza business to create an international operation training and consulting to business owners and managers. Robert asked me to conduct training sessions at his Business School for Entrepreneurs in Hawaii later that year. That was July 1994, and 350 business owners from around the world and 11 trainers (mostly in their 40's and 50's) were there to learn from me!

That was pretty heady stuff for me at the time and it meant I would have to concentrate 100% of my time and effort on it if I was to complete this assignment successfully. There was only one thing to do – I had to find a business partner who could run my business affairs back home while I was presenting seminars, consulting and basically generating cashflow.

Once that was in place, I then proceeded to present literally hundreds of seminars all over Australia, New Zealand, Asia and the United States.

I arrived back home in January 1995 to find that, not only was I extremely tired, sick of travel, and missing the routine of regular business, but I was also actually broke.

And so I learnt my very first major business lesson; partnerships don't always work.

I suddenly found myself seriously in debt – to the tune of a few million dollars! I had no option but to move back into my parents' house.

At first I was devastated. I found it difficult to get motivated and wondered what on earth I was going to do to get out of this mess. Do you want to know what the scariest thing was at the time? I almost went out and got a job. Even though I'd just spent the last 11 months teaching everyone else how to make money, I spent three full days just sitting quietly wondering why I couldn't seem to do the same for myself. At the time I thought that life could never get any worse.

Then my Dad came in one day and said, "You can't just sit there moping; get out and do something to sort this out."

That was it – I suddenly had the motivation I was looking for. The first thing I did was to get a phone line connected. Then I put a desk next to my bed and started all over again.

I sent a letter to every one of my past clients, seminar attendees and everyone else I knew, offering my consulting services once more. After a few solid days on the phone, I was back in business. I sat down and wrote out the Vision, Mission and Culture Statement of the new company I was going to create. I had decided to stay in the business of training business owners, but this time I'd be sure to do it well.

This is what I came up with:

Action International

Business Coaching that's Guaranteed
to Improve Your Performance ...

The Vision You'll Support ...

World Abundance through Business Re-education ...

The Mission Statement You'll Embody ...

Action International is a team of committed, positive and successful people who are always striving to be balanced, integrated and honest. We will work within our *"12 Points of Culture"* to make sure that everyone who touches or is touched by the *Action* International team will benefit greatly and in some way move closer to becoming the person they want to be or achieve the goals they want to achieve.

We will always work in co-opetition with all those who believe they are in competition with us.

We are in the business of Edutainment. We will educate ourselves, our clients and all those whom we work with, whilst we entertain them and create a fun learning environment. We will educate our clients in world-class marketing and business development techniques using audio, video, CD's, other technologies and simple workbooks, workshops and seminar formats.

Our products and services will be of the highest quality, value for money and whether sourced from within the company or externally will always add the most value and use the latest and most effective training methodologies available.

Action International clients whether they be small, medium or large in size will have a desire to have us help them in achieving their goals and be able to take on Our Commitment to them by returning their Commitment to *Action*. They will be forward thinking, willing to learn and grow, and be willing to work as a team player in the development of an organisation of 'people'.

Our clients will be selected more on attitude than size and they will want to deal with us because we understand people are important, systems should run a company, we offer the most practical, most applicable and fastest strategies of growth and most importantly because we mean what we say.

We will give people back their spirit and freedom through business development.

The Uniqueness You'll Help to Position *Action* *International* with ...

The World's Most Practical Marketing and Business Development because Being in Business should Give You More life ...

Action's 12 Points of Culture ...

Commitment - You will be committed to the Vision, Mission, Goals and Rules and SUCCESS of *Action International,* its current and future team, and its clients at all times.

- You will always recommend products and services of *Action* International prior to going outside the company.

Ownership - Accept that you as an individual are truly responsible for your actions and outcomes and own everything that takes place in your work and your life.

Integrity - You will always speak the truth. What you promise is what you deliver.

- You will only ever make agreements you are willing and intend to keep.

- You will communicate any potential broken agreements at the first opportunity.

- You will clear up all broken agreements immediately.

Excellence - Good enough isn't. You will always deliver products of exceptional quality that add value to all involved for the long term.

- You will look for ways to do more with less and stay on a path of constant and never ending improvement and innovation.

Communication - You will always speak positively of your team members, your clients and *Action* International in both public and private.

- You will speak with good purpose using empowering and positive conversation.

- You will never use or listen to profanity, sarcasm or gossip.

- You will acknowledge what is being said as true for the speaker at that moment.

- You will take responsibility for responses to your communication.

- You will greet and farewell people using their name.

- You will always apologise for any upsets first ... and then look for a solution.

- You will only ever discuss concerns in private with the person involved.

Success
- You will focus your attention on the successful outcome of whatever you are doing.

- You will have a willingness to win and allow others to win ... win/win.

- You will display pride, prosperity, competence and personal confidence.

Education
- You will always be willing to learn from your mistakes.

- You will always be striving to learn, grow and master so you can help your fellow team members and clients learn, grow and master too.

- You will act as an educator to allow your clients to make their own intelligent decisions about their future remembering that it is their future.

- You will impart practical, useable knowledge rather than just theory.

Team Work
- You will be willing to do whatever it takes to stay together and achieve team goals.

- You will focus on co-operation and always come to a resolution, not a compromise.

- You'll be flexible in your work, able to change if what you're doing's not working.

- You will ask for help when you need it and be compassionate to others who ask you.

Balance
- You will have a balanced approach to life remembering that your spiritual, social, physical and family aspects are just as important as your financial and intellectual.

Fun
- You view life as a journey to be enjoyed and appreciated and will help to create an atmosphere of fun and happiness so all around you enjoy it as well.

Systems
- You will always look to the system for a solution. If a problem arises you will look for a system correction before you look for a people correction.

- You will look for a system solution in your innovation rather than a people solution.

- You will follow the system exactly until a new system is introduced.

- You will suggest system improvements at your first opportunity.

Consistency
- You will be consistent in your actions so that your customers can feel comfortable in dealing with you at all times.

In March of that year my best friend from University began working with me. We worked from my parents' 'granny flat'. I recorded sets of tapes while doing the seminars, kept selling and consulting during the day, and continued selling the tapes. We stayed back until about ten or eleven each night planning and systemising. We were preparing the groundwork for a business that could be replicated time and time again. In essence, we were preparing to franchise the business.

It wasn't long before I'd paid back everything I owed, saved a few dollars, and had a plan in place to create an amazing worldwide organisation. To cut a long story short, within three years and after many trials and tribulations, I managed to create a company called *Action International*. I had employed 24 people in Australia to take care of the business in Australia and New Zealand. A joint venture deal (worth several millions of dollars) was then signed to open an office in Singapore to service South East Asia and in 1998 I felt everything was in place to enable me to take the big decision to go global through franchising.

It had been a whirlwind couple of years, with over 188,000 people attending *Action* seminars, 14,300 participating in my intensive workshops, and 397 businesses benefiting from *Action* consulting services.

So what did we do to prepare the company for franchising?

I first sat down and developed a set of personal goals, which was what I called the Brad Sugars' Entrepreneurs Credo. This is what it contained:

Be organised. Schedule a written program of your activities and objectives and stick with it the entire day.

Be dedicated. Do at least one thing every day that you should have done, but have been putting off.

Be confident. Feel as good as possible and achieve a sense of well being by meditating at least 15 minutes every day. Exercise for another 15 minutes every day.

Be appreciative. Tell your family, friends and business associates how much you appreciate them every week. Be generous with your praise and compliments.

Be optimistic. Leave past failures in the past, and think and focus positively on your future.

Be educated. Read something that will improve your mind every day. Keep yourself away from non-productive people, activities and news.

Be thrifty. Never pay full price, consume less and never pay any more tax than is absolutely necessary.

Be sociable. Be charming and agreeable, never speak badly of anyone.

Be alert. Open yourself to new ideas, experiences and people who can teach you something new. Stay out of ruts and routines.

Be dependable. Meet all of your business, social and moral obligations punctually, honestly and honourably.

Be decisive. Make the decision right now.

Be human. Remember to experience the journey as well as the results.

Be tough. Demand only the highest and the best standards of everyone you surround yourself with.

Give and you shall receive.

These 14 points became the belief system that guided the way I lived through each and every day. This became my system of personal principles or beliefs. Sure it took time to replace the old set of beliefs, but by working at it slowly and focusing on each one every single day, I was soon able to adopt them so that they became my guiding light.

They became my '14 Commandments'. I was amazed at how powerful they were once I began following them. And best of all, once they had become second nature to me, they actually began to make the work I was doing to establish a franchise business, all the more easier. Suddenly, things that would previously have seemed a huge challenge were tackled with ease. My team felt happier, more empowered and assured that contributions were indeed appreciated. Outsiders picked this up too, and would comment at the unique atmosphere within our company. It was fantastic.

Encouraged by this, and with a new lease on life, I sat down and wrote out a document that detailed what I called my categories and roles. This is what I committed to:

Category: Physical Body

Role: Healthy athlete and work-out king

Category: Spiritual Life

Role: Amazing God-like being

Category: Emotional Life

Role: Creator of my own meanings, feelings and experiences

Role: Giver of amazing experiences

Category: Friendships

Role: Fun-loving, inspirational and reliable buddy

Category: Family

Role: Loving son and amazing, inspirational brother

Role: Supportive, loving and exciting best friend to my partner

Category: Personal Development

Role: Growth King and Super Learner

Role: Seeker and Creator of exciting new learning opportunities

Category: Contribution

Role: Provider to the community, Founder of the Brad Sugars Trust

Category: Good Life

Role: Creator of amazingly, wonderful, balancing events

Category: Financial Freedom

Role: Skilled, highly successful, wealth producing, positive cashflow asset acquirer

Role: Super, money managing, high ROI producing, tax minimising multi-millionaire

Category: Business

Role: In demand business presenter, educator and amazing facilitator

Role: Supportive, intelligent and unreasonable business partner

Role: Chairman, key strategist & presenter for *Action* International Pty Ltd

Role: Chairman, key strategist & presenter for *Action* Australia Ltd

Role: Chairman, key strategist & presenter for *Action* International (Asia) Pte Ltd

Role: Partner, key strategist & trainer for Trophy Dog Food and Associated Companies

Role: Partner & key sponsorship creator for Teardrop Pty Ltd & Lifeline

Role: Chairman & key strategist for On-Hold Action Pty Ltd

Role: Chairman & key strategist for Co-opetition Pty Ltd

Role: Chairman & key strategist for Geoffrey Johns Group Pty Ltd

Role: Chairman & key strategist for QBN Properties Pty Ltd

Role: Chairman & key strategist for L&B Hairdressing Pty Ltd

Role: Creator of best-selling learning tools and education programs

Role: Acquisition monster, opportunity spotter and business turnaround expert

Role: International best-selling author

Role: Highly called upon business and media personality

I had set myself clear, and challenging, goals. I had a vision. And I had stopped dreaming. You see, my dream was taking on the appearance of reality. I was actually beginning to live my dream.

My team and I then set about developing systems that were based on the tried and tested methodologies that we had used to great effect during the previous couple of years. Let's now look at some of these in greater detail.

Due to the nature of what the company does – business coaching – we would definitely fit the definition of a Business Format Franchise. What we would be selling would be a comprehensive system that our franchisees would follow to the letter to achieve results for their clients. We would be selling a system that would include absolutely everything from business planning to management tools, and from computer systems to training and backup. Consistency and uniformity were to be major hallmarks of our system.

What followed were long days and even longer nights, but we had a lot of fun. We brainstormed, developed drafts, discarded them and started again, and refined each system after testing and measuring, before finally coming up with something that we were happy with.

These are the systems we developed:

- Sales systems
- Business presentation system
- Consultant's training system
- Business Coach's system
- Sales system
- Accounts system
- Stock ordering system

Of course, this wasn't the end of it. We wrote manuals for each system as well as Key Performance Indicators for each and every position.

But let's get into some of the detail here. This should give you a better idea of what's involved in developing these systems.

The Business Coach's system included an Ultimate Marketing Plan. This was what it involved, from a development point-of-view:

- First Contact Script
- Welcome System – fax and kit
- 12 Month Goals
- 4 Day Workshop/Calendar/Booking Forms
- Progress Checklist
- Alignment Template
- Plan Of *Action* (SWOT Box)
- Video/Book Schedule
- Testing And Measuring Systems
- Consultation Booking Schedule
- Client Consultation Scripts
- Client Monthly Formula
- Copywriter's Brief
- Consultation Goals
- Critique Forms
- Results Forms
- Coach Piece Check Forms
- Congratulations System
- Monthly Progress Report
- Quarterly Progress Report
- Phone Scripts
- PERT Goals
- Mission Statement

Each system contained details of every aspect of that function you could possibly imagine. You see, the secret is to write everything down in the finest of detail so that ANYONE could do that job if they were given the manual. These systems become the very lifeblood of the company. And because companies must, by their very nature, grow as time passes, the systems too evolve as circumstances change. Remember, business is like a tree; it is either growing or it is dying. Staying the same is not an option.

Our systems changed as circumstances changed. Systems need to be dynamic to succeed. And that's really the beauty of them. That way, if a problem arises in the business, you focus first on fixing the system rather than zeroing in on the hapless person. This way you avoid, to a large extent, all those nasty and destructive personnel issues that so often sour previously harmonious companies. One of our key contentions is that systems should run the company, while people run the systems.

Today when a person buys an *Action* franchise they receive everything they'll need to get into business in the quickest possible time to start generating business and cashflow. They are sent away on a comprehensive live-in training course that lasts ten days. They also receive the following set of six manuals:

Initial Training: Getting Into Your *Action* Business

Kickstart: Getting Your Business Into *Action*

Marketing: Building Your Inquiry Funnel

Sales: Converting Your Inquiry

Alignment: Getting Your Clients Focused

Coaching: Building Your Client's Business

Master Licensees receive, in addition to the above list, a **Master Licensees Manual**. We also supply them with a **Business Development Manager's Manual**.

All this is backed up with a state-of-the-art internet-based "Member's Directory," which is an on-line powerhouse of knowledge, business resources, communication tools and a discussion forum.

We've come a long way in an incredibly short period of time. In just nine short years, we've spread our wings and operate out of offices in Australia, New Zealand, USA, UK, Ireland, Malaysia, Singapore, China and Mexico. Our Global Head Office is in Brisbane, Australia.

And we've had our fair share of challenges along the way. Some of them were what one would expect from any rapidly expanding business, and others were more taxing – like having to go through the traumatic, and costly, exercise of changing our entire USA management team during 2001/2.

My current goal is to sell 2005 franchises by the year 2005. Ambitious maybe, but so far we are on track to achieve that.

> The quality of your life is determined by the quality of the decisions you make, which is determined by the quality of questions you ask, which is determined by the quality of your education.
>
> ***Brad Sugars***

▮ Humble Beginnings – The Birth Of A New Way Of Doing Business

Did you know? ...

The town of Evanston, Illinois was known as being so religious-minded in the late 19th Century that it was nicknamed Heavenston. They passed an ordinance forbidding the sale of ice cream sodas on Sundays. Not wanting to be hard done by or to break the law, enterprising businessmen then started serving the ice cream with syrup instead of soda. These Sunday sodas, as they became known, were so popular that people started demanding them on other days of the week as well and not just on Sundays. The town fathers then objected to the product being named after the Sabbath, so the businessmen changed the spelling to Sundae.

The simple ice cream and milk shake may have a lot to answer for. You see, not only did they evolve into one of the most quintessential of all American icons; they've also got a lot to do with the birth of a whole new way of doing business. You see, they were at the centre of the evolution of a new business system that became known as franchising.

This amazing story began back in 1925 with a man named Howard Johnson.

Who was Howard Johnson? Howard Dearing Johnson was one of those rare human beings who see their destiny, and have the drive, the talent, and the imagination to seize it. He set out to make a name for himself - and didn't rest until that name had become one of the world's great brands, and one of the best-known landmarks in travel.

He not only built one of the first great restaurant chains and one of the first mid-price hotel chains, he pioneered many of the most successful food service and hospitality innovations. The franchisee ownership concept, the turnpike restaurant concept, the super premium ice cream concept, the 'Theme' restaurant concept, the commissary food distribution concept, the 'America's Menu' concept, the quality motor lodge concept, the 'Kids-Go-Free' family travel concept - they are all classic examples of the business and marketing genius of Howard Johnson.

It's a great American success story - and it all began at a small town soda fountain.

In 1925, Howard Johnson borrowed $2,000 to buy a small corner drugstore in Wollaston, Massachusetts. It sold candy, newspapers and patent medicine - but Howard quickly noticed that the real action was at his old marble soda fountain. He figured that if he could invent a better tasting ice cream cone, the world (or at least Wollaston) would beat a path to the Howard Johnson store.

He came up with a 'secret formula' for vanilla and chocolate ice cream. The secret was, in fact, based on his mother's recipe for ice cream - with all natural ingredients and twice the normal butterfat content. It was an immediate sensation, so he quickly added other flavours. He had invented a super premium ice cream.

When summer came, he opened a beachfront ice cream stand, and that first summer he sold $60,000 worth of ice cream cones - at a nickel a cone. By 1928 he was selling $240,000 worth of ice cream cones. He kept adding flavours until he reached 28 varieties.

"I thought I had every flavour in the world," Howard remarked. "The 28 flavours became my trademark." He advertised it, truthfully, as 'New England's Best Ice Cream,' and his success reinforced what became the guiding principle of his business life: Quality sells.

Over the next few summers he added more beachfront stands, and decided to do for the lowly hot dog what he had done for the ice cream cone. Instead of using the normal hot dog stand method of slapping them on a greasy grill, and then wrapping them in stale buns, he invented the idea of clipping the frankfurters at both ends, notching them lengthwise, and then cooking them in pure creamery butter that would infuse into the meat. He used only the highest quality meats (unheard of in those days) and lightly toasted, buttered fresh rolls. He had elevated the hot dog to connoisseur status, and it was to become one of the unforgettable joys of visiting Howard Johnson's restaurants for generations. Again, that little extra drive for quality would pay enormous dividends in the years to come.

His success was beginning to be noticed by others, and so he was able to convince some sceptical bankers to lend him enough money to open a restaurant in Quincy, Massachusetts. It was located in Quincy's first skyscraper – a ten-story granite art deco building that still looks magnificent today. This first Howard Johnson's restaurant featured fried clams, baked beans, chicken pies, those elegant frankfurters, and, of course, the now locally famous Howard Johnson ice cream. He was restless to expand - but the stock market crashed, the Depression began, and the banks weren't lending money.

Then Howard had a remarkable idea, one that would change the course of American business enterprise. In 1935, he persuaded an acquaintance to open another 'Howard Johnson's' restaurant in Orleans on Cape Cod under a franchise. Howard Johnson would design the space, create the menu, set the standards, and deliver the food and ice cream. The franchisee, under a license, would own the property and receive the bulk of the revenues. Howard, always a stickler for quality, demanded that the restaurant be run by his quality standards, or the contract was void and the franchisee would have to remove the Howard Johnson sign.

Seemingly overnight, out of the depths of the Depression, a phenomenal business success was born. By the following summer there were 17 Howard Johnson's restaurants. All were successful beyond anyone's wildest expectations. Paul Herbert, for instance, opened a 70-seat restaurant in Cambridge, putting up $10,000 as one-third the cost, the remainder to be financed over three years. Mr. Herbert hoped he would gross $60,000 a year, but he actually grossed $200,000 during the first 12 months. It was something of an understatement when he declared, "You're in a good business when you own a Howard Johnson franchise."

That sentiment was to be repeated by many hundreds of happy and wealthy franchisees. By the end of 1936 there were 39 more franchised restaurants.

Howard Johnson moved with lightning speed, for he had seen that the growing popularity of the automobile was sending millions of hungry Americans out on the road, and there were no decent places to satisfy their needs. He created the highway landmark concept, featuring the bright orange roof and the Simple Simon and the Pie Man road sign. By 1939 there were 107 Howard Johnson restaurants along East Coast highways generating revenues of $10.5 million.

All were run according to the 'Howard Johnson Bible' - a set of strict standards of cleanliness, service, recipes, menu items and quality (as well as interior and exterior design) that were developed and rigidly enforced by Howard Johnson himself. It was quite a voluminous bible, and it left nothing to chance. The author meticulously wrote every instruction on everything and anything that had to do with the running of his restaurants. He would allow no variation from one restaurant to the other. One chapter was devoted to the 'Howard Johnson Waitresses - Your Appearance from Head to Toe.' An entire page covered the subject of being courteous, including instructions on how to 'assist customers with their wraps.'

As the vast American highway system began to span the continent, millions of travellers, in their Ford 'woody' station wagons and Chevy coupes, eagerly searched for the familiar orange roof and the big Howard Johnson sign with Simple Simon and the Pie Man on top.

They searched, and the kids clapped and cheered when they saw it, for they all knew exactly what they would find inside - the best fried clams anywhere, hot dogs grilled in butter and served on toasted rolls, old-fashioned chicken pot pie, generous turkey dinners with mashed potatoes, moist rich brownies, games and puzzles for the kids, high chairs for the tots, and 28 flavours of the world's best ice cream. All served family style, by smiling waitresses in their prim, starched blue and orange dresses, all to be enjoyed in spanking clean, colourful surroundings.

Here was the nation's 'Host of the Highway,' where everyone invariably found a warm welcome, a familiar experience, and a special feeling that became part of growing up in America.

In less than 14 years, the dreamer who aspired to create a better ice cream cone now directed a mammoth franchise network of over 10,000 employees, with 170 restaurants, many serving a million and a half people a year.

And the heady beat went on.

The Pennsylvania, Ohio and New Jersey turnpikes were built, and Howard Johnson bid and won exclusive rights to serve the hungry turnpike multitudes. There were 200 Howard Johnson restaurants on the morning that America woke up to three huge black letters on the front page: WAR!

With World War II came gas rationing, food stamps and the end of pleasure trips. One by one, the restaurants were forced to close. By the summer of 1944, only 12 remained in business. Howard managed to stay barely afloat by serving commissary food to war workers and army recruits. But by the time America was celebrating V-J Day, Howard Johnson was working late into the nights getting ready for the travel boom and the highway expansion that he knew had to be coming.

He was about to make one of the biggest comebacks in business history. After the war, America turned its incredible energy to building houses in a new world called 'suburbia,' building big, powerful cars that seemingly everyone could afford, and building the endless interstate highway system that connected the cities and the people, coast to coast. It was a world custom-made for our 'pioneer of the highways' Howard Johnson. And he didn't waste a minute.

By 1947, construction was under way or about to begin on 200 new Howard Johnson restaurants that would stretch across the Southeast and Midwest. These were slightly smaller buildings than the pre-war originals, but Howard Johnson still provided over 700 items, including his famous fried clams, saltwater taffy and 28 flavours of ice cream. By 1951, Howard Johnson sales totalled $115 million.

By 1954, there were 400 Howard Johnson restaurants in 32 states. About 10% were company-owned turnpike restaurants that were extremely profitable. The orange roof just kept spreading until it rivalled Coca-

Cola's trademark as the most familiar icon in America. And countless memories of family travel were born under every orange roof.

In 1959, the company founder, who still made his headquarters in Wollaston, Massachusetts, decided it was time to turn the reins over to his son, 26 year old Howard Brennon Johnson, who succeeded him as president. Young Howard, a graduate of Andover and Yale, told a reporter, "I knew from the age of five that I wanted to join the company. It was all we talked about at home. And my father was the kind of person you almost couldn't let down." The senior Howard Johnson remained as chairman and treasurer, though he was now able to enjoy his sixty-foot yacht and his growing art collection. He died in 1972, at the age of 76.

According to the International Franchise Association, most analysts estimate that franchising companies and their franchisees accounted for $1 trillion in annual US retail sales from 320,000 franchised small businesses in 75 industries.

Franchising in Australia is a fairly recent phenomenon and was virtually unknown until the 1970s, when the major US fast-food franchise systems began infiltrating the market. Big names such as Pizza Hut and KFC were among the first to introduce this dynamic new method of conducting business to the locals. Since then, the business format franchising system in particular has grown tremendously in Australia and now pervades virtually every product and service. Today the social, economic and commercial significance of the franchise system cannot be ignored in Australia.

Over the past 20 years, franchising as an alternative means of either starting a new business or expanding an existing one, has become increasingly popular as more and more foreign franchises invaded the market. Of course, many Australian companies are not far behind, with their own home-grown marketing techniques proving to be successful business models, better suited to the Australian economic climate.

The franchising concept has provided many small Australian retailers with the competitive resources they need to hold their positions against the larger retailers. Although the franchise system started out as a source for foreign products and structures, many Australians have now chosen to adopt a local franchise system. In fact, the majority of franchise systems in this country are now Australian-owned, and an increasing number of them are successfully taking their concepts offshore.

"When all is said and done, franchising is all about relationships."

Brad Sugars

▐ What Is Franchising?

Did you know? ... _____

Pizza Hut opened their first company owned restaurant in Wichita, Kansas, in 1958.

Pizza Hut opened their first franchise unit in Topeka, Kansas in 1959.

Pizza Hut opened their first restaurant in Australia in 1970.

Mention the word franchising to anyone and chances are they'll immediately think of names such as Subway, KFC and Pizza Hut. Funny how the 'big guys', the internationals, always seem to spring to mind first. Then, after some reflection, names like Harvey Norman, Kwik Kopy and VIP Home Services will roll off their lips. These are the larger, home-grown, true blue, Aussie success stories that everyone is familiar with. And then, of course, there is the local lawn mowing service that is well and truly a part of our local suburban scene.

But franchising goes far deeper than that. It is alive and well and operating in almost every business category in the economy, from banking to petroleum supplies, and from legal services to dog washing. One could almost be forgiven for thinking that franchising is the very cornerstone of the economy!

So what is franchising? Does a succinct definition exist?

A franchise can be defined as:

- Authorisation given to somebody to sell or distribute a company's goods or services in a particular area.

- A business or group of businesses set up or operated specifically in accordance with an authorisation.

- The territory or the limits within which the right to operate a business exists.

- A professional sports team.

Well, modern day sporting teams are big business, aren't they?

The word franchise is actually a very old one, originating back in the 14th Century, believe it or not. It meant free, or to make free. Isn't that interesting? If you think about it, the meaning has changed over time. It could be argued that today, it has acquired almost the opposite meaning!

This is how the Franchise Council of Australia describes franchising: Franchising is not a business itself, but a way of doing business. It is essentially a marketing concept – an innovative method of distributing goods and services. It is also an extremely successful and rapidly growing aspect of Australia's small business sector.

But like everything in life, it's not as simple as it first appears. Franchising, it goes on to explain, is used to describe a number of business models, the most common being *business format franchising*. But there are other models that are also dependent on franchise relationships. These include:

1. Manufacturer-Retailer: where the retailer as a franchisee sells the franchisor's product directly to the public, such as new motor vehicle dealership.

2. Manufacturer-Wholesaler: where the franchisee, under license, manufactures and distributes the franchisor's product, such as in soft drink bottling arrangements.

3. Wholesaler-Retailer: where the retailer as a franchisee purchases products for retail sale from a franchisor wholesaler, such as in hardware and automotive product stores.

4. Retailer-Retailer: where the franchisor markets a service or a product under a common name and standardised system through a network of franchisees. This is the classic business format franchise.

In essence, franchising is a relationship between the franchisor: (the company selling the franchise) and the franchisee: (the person buying the franchise). Franchisees usually pay a franchise fee as well as royalties for their franchise, but more about this later.

Because franchising is a very unique way of doing business, and it covers a very diverse range of businesses – some big and some small – the only way of ensuring the system doesn't self-destruct is to create a peak industry body to oversee virtually every facet of its operation. In Australia, this body is the Franchise Council of Australia, which represents franchisees, franchisors and service providers to the sector. Its objectives are:

- To establish standards of international best practice in business format franchising for Australian franchise systems.

- To provide information and education about franchising to existing and potential franchisees and franchisors.

- To lobby state and federal governments on issues relevant to the sector.

- To develop a vital, strong and financially viable franchising sector.

- To advance the interests of members in Australia and in special interest markets such as the International Franchise Community, Franchise Advisory Councils, Small Business Forums and property leasing organisations (particularly shopping centres).

- To continually foster among consumers, governments and the business community, a broad-based understanding of the economic importance of having a strong franchising sector in Australia

- To design efficient, identified, value-added services to members and assist them to be more effective in franchising.

As the peak body for franchising in Australia, the Franchise Council of Australia continues to add value to the businesses of its members by providing a range of services relevant to franchising and which represent good value. It is closely affiliated with franchising associations around the world, and is a founding member of the Asia Pacific Franchise Confederation. It is also a member of the World Franchise Council.

A Code of Conduct regulates the affairs of the industry, which is a mandatory industry code that regulates the conduct of participants in franchising towards other participants in franchising. In relation to franchise agreements concerning the retail marketing of motor fuel, it operates concurrently with the Petroleum Retail Marketing Franchise Act 1980. The Code covers everything from disclosure to conditions for franchise agreement and dispute resolution. The Federal Government amended the Franchising Code of Conduct by introducing the Trade Practices (Industry Code - Franchising Amendment) Regulations 2001. The Regulations were made by the Governor General on the 28th of June 2001 and commenced on the 1st of October 2001.

So now you have a general idea of what franchising is all about. And you should also realise that it is a complex field that has many variations and permutations – no two franchise systems are exactly the same.

Let's now take a closer look at the scope and scale of franchising, and what it means to the economy. I'm talking big picture here. This should put franchising in perspective.

> "Franchising brings a great business idea together with people who have both the capital and the passion to run the business."
>
> *Brad Sugars*

▋ How Big Is The Industry?

Did you know? ... _____

Australia is the most franchised nation per head of population in the world. That is, there are more franchise systems in Australia compared to our population than any other country, and Australia has at least three times as many franchise systems per head of population than the United States. *(Franchising Australia 2002, the Commonwealth Bank Franchising Survey)*

Franchising is an industry that is alive, well and growing at a phenomenal rate. Its tentacles have spread into just about every corner of our economy. But perhaps more importantly, there are very clear indications that the industry is maturing. Gone are the days when franchising was generally regarded with deep suspicion by the average Australian. Sure there were some quite spectacular crashes and many people lost a lot of money, but since then regulations have been instituted to ensure, as far as possible, that dubious practices remain a thing of the past.

According to Franchise Council of Australia Chairman, Stephen Giles, it is now beyond rational argument that franchising delivers a competitive advantage to the franchisors and franchisees that embrace best practice franchising principles in their business. "The franchise sector delivers $80 billion in annual turnover, employs 500,000 people, has around 420,000 permanent employees, generates $292 million in annual export earnings, and has 90% of its business owners earning profits beyond wages. These are stunning figures."

Stunning figures indeed. But let's put this in perspective. Let's look at the background against which the industry returned these figures. No, I'm not talking about the economic conditions or state of the nation, but the internal state of the franchise industry. You see, it's vitally important to understand what the state of the players were when they put in this record-breaking performance. Commenting on the results of the 2002 Commonwealth Bank Franchising Survey, Stephen Giles said: "It is pleasing to see that less than 1% of franchisees were involved in a 'substantial dispute' with their franchisor, meaning a dispute involving litigation, mediation or correspondence with a solicitor. 81% of franchisors recorded no substantial disputes at all in their system in the past 12 months. These are important statistics for those thinking of buying a franchise, and further signs of the increased maturity of the sector."

Isn't that interesting?

So let's take a closer look at the industry in Australia. According to the most recent data (September 2002), there are some 700 different franchise systems operating in Australia. That's three times as many per head of population than in the USA. Take a moment to think about this – it's quite staggering. Think about the influence franchising has on our economy. Think about how many families rely on it for their livelihoods.

Now here's another thing you will find astonishing. Over 90% of these 700 franchise systems are true blue Australian. Isn't that something! I'd say this is a good indication that the industry has reached a certain level of maturity.

Here's something else that may come as a surprise. The average Australian franchisor has been in business for 15 years, nine of which have been as a franchise.

There are now almost 50,000 franchise outlets operating in Australia. That's 8.5% up on 1999 figures. Something else that indicates that the industry has reached maturity is that the average number of franchised units per franchise has doubled in the last three years.

But of course, we can't just judge the state or importance of the industry in terms of absolute numbers. You see, we might well have 50,000 franchise outlets operating in this country, but what if they were, on average, operating in the red? What would be the use of that?

Are they making money? How profitable are they? That's the big question.

Of course, it would be just about impossible to give indicative figures here, but what I can say is that franchising is big business, especially in terms of the all important export dollar. The best information I have indicates that $292 million is generated from the overseas operations of Australian franchisors each year. And that's from a relatively small base. You see, only 25% of Australian franchisors have expanded into overseas markets.

Where are these markets? Not surprisingly, the biggest is New Zealand, where 74% of our franchisors do business. Next comes the UK at 36%, followed by the USA and Singapore at 34%, and South Africa and Europe at 26%. It's also interesting to note that 62% of Australian franchisors say they intend opening operations abroad within the next three years. Just think what that will do to our balance of payments if even half manage to take the plunge.

OK, so what about the franchise scene at home? How big is it? How many people earn a living in the industry?

It's quite staggering, really. According to the Commonwealth Bank Franchising Survey of 2002, the franchise industry now employs approximately 500,000 people. But here's another important indicator: of those leaving the industry, 74% was due to the successful sale of their franchise. This shows that franchising not only provides a decent livelihood, but it also is a good investment. It is more than just a job.

In monetary terms, the annual turnover of the franchise industry within Australia is $78 billion. That's 12% of GDP! The overwhelming feeling is that franchise businesses in Australia are affordable, with the average start-up cost for a mobile business being $62,500 and $208,000 for a fixed location franchise. But here's the interesting part: 90% of franchisees believe they earn profit over and above employee wages. This figure compares extremely favourably with the small business sector.

OK, so what's the situation across the Tasman? How big is franchising in New Zealand?

According to the 2001 Franchising Association of New Zealand Survey of Franchising, the industry is worth around $10 billion. There are over 300 franchise systems operating there, with some 77% of them being home-grown. Franchising employs approximately 70,000 people.

The Franchise Association of New Zealand plays an important role in the New Zealand economy, promoting a Code of Practice and a Code of Ethics by which all its members must abide. You see, New Zealand does not have any specific legislation in relation to franchising, although franchised businesses are subject to normal commercial law. The Association's Codes provide for full disclosure of information to potential franchisees in order to allow them to make realistic and informed decisions. Although it has to be said, this level of protection is only available through dealing with members of the Association.

Even though the industry is not as large as it is in Australia, it is still an important part of the economy. And rightly so. Many New Zealand franchisors are now firmly establishing themselves in overseas markets; Fastway Couriers, The Fish Shop and the Entrepreneurs Success Centre are just a few examples.

Interestingly enough, only 16% of respondents to the 2001 survey did not consider that the franchise provided a good return on investment for the franchisor (and 6% for the franchisee), with 31% of respondents rating their system as excellent and 46% as above average. According to Robert Fowler, Chairman of the Franchise Association of New Zealand, the survey confirms the upward trend for franchising in New Zealand, with growth in new systems, growth in turnover and growth in employment. "With these sorts of results it is easy to see why franchising has become such a worldwide success story, and that is because people in franchising are reaping the rewards."

"Most businesses that fail in franchising do so because they don't have the margin for the franchisees to take off a profit after the franchise fee."

Brad Sugars

▌ The Nature Of Franchising

Did you know? ... _____

The Athlete's Foot was established in 1971 in Pittsburgh Pennsylvania. It is the world's first, and largest, franchisor of athletic footwear.

The Athlete's Foot is a privately owned subsidiary of Groupe Rallye, a French food retail conglomerate that has interests in fashion, home improvements, sport and real estate.

The Athlete's Foot has 750 stores in 45 countries, including 96 in Australia and New Zealand. The first Australian store was opened in Adelaide in 1979.

Not all franchise systems are the same. Seems like an obvious observation, but there's more to it than meets the eye. Just because a company has chosen the franchise route doesn't mean its basic way of operating or conducting business will be the same as other franchises.

This is one of the common misconceptions about franchising. To be successful in the world of franchising, this is the very first thing you need to understand.

Think of it like baking a cake. There are many different recipes you could use to bake a cake. They all have the same objective in mind – a cake. But they probably take different routes. You see, one may call for the ingredients to be mixed and then placed in the microwave oven. Another might use the same ingredients, only this time they are to be placed in a cake tin in the oven. Yet others may use pre-mixed ingredients, and all you need to do is to add water. But they all produce the same cake. Now we could go further and say that some recipes are for chocolate cakes while others are for cream sponge cakes. But I think you get the idea.

Franchising is the same. There are various routes a franchised business can take to profitability. There are different business recipes it can follow. These are called models.

The interesting thing to note about these different models is that they hinge around the differing relationships that exist between the franshisor and the franchisee. And remember, in franchising, these relationships are fundamental to the ultimate success or failure of the business experience.

OK, so what are these models?

Modern franchising revolves around two main models; Product/Trade Name Franchises and the Business Format Franchise. There are others, and those will be discussed briefly a little later on. First, let's have a closer look at the two major types.

Product/Trade Name Franchises

When you come to think of it, the very reason for existing for many businesses is to sell a product or a range of products. It's the product that occupies centre stage here.

Let's take the motor industry as an example. The Ford Motor Company manufacturers a range of motor vehicles to satisfy particular motoring needs in the market. How does it get these vehicles to its customers? Does it sell them directly to the motoring public? No, it supplies stock to motor dealerships, which do the selling. They are the middlemen that become the 'face' of the company as far as the buying public is concerned. It is the dealership that the customer has contact with.

These dealerships 'look' as though they are part of the Ford Motor Company, but they aren't. You see, although they display all the outward appearances of the Ford Motor Company, they are in actual fact privately owned franchises of the Ford Motor Company.

It's primarily the product and the trade name that are paramount here. These are the visible manifestations of the business arrangement.

So what are the important features of a product/trademark franchise? It all comes down to the type, or nature, of the business relationship that exists between the franchisor on the one hand and the franchisee on the other.

In these instances, the franchisor remains very much more relaxed about the way in which the franchisee goes about selling its product. This does not mean there are little or no operational standards that must be met – there are – but the franchisee is very much more in control of these functions than in other models.

The franchisor usually derives profit from the ongoing supply of the product to its franchisees and from the upfront fee payable to secure the rights to sell the product and use the trade name in the first place. Advice and ongoing support in the areas of product knowledge, training, service, advertising and promotion is usually also supplied to franchisees.

Now if you had a Product/Trade Name franchise, it wouldn't necessarily mean that you were a middleman or a distributor. You could be a manufacturer too, manufacturing a franchisor's product under licence. This is a very popular arrangement, especially in the food and beverage sector. The product would still be the major focal point and the franchisee would still enjoy a very high level of independence. Soft drink bottling companies are a good example.

Business Format Franchise

The other major franchise model is known as the Business Format Franchise. This is the model that most people would be thinking of when the word franchise is mentioned. This is, of course, purely coincidental, because most people wouldn't really know what distinguishes the one model from the other. Let's hope that in a few minutes time, you won't be able to count yourself as one of them!

This type of franchise is, according to the Franchise Council of Australia, the fastest growing type in the Australian franchise industry. So what are the main distinguishing characteristics of this model then?

For starters, the relationship between the franchisor and the franchisee is very much more rigid. It is very much more prescribed. You see, when someone buys one of these franchises, they are buying a complete and comprehensive system. You see, the franchisor has developed not only a great product, but also an entire and comprehensive system through which to take it to market. The franchisee is, therefore, buying not only the right to sell the product and make use of the trade name or trademark, but also goodwill, product and marketing knowledge, intellectual property, marketing and promotion power, ongoing training, quality control, operational policies and procedures, research and development, assistance, guidance, support and bulk buying muscle. This is very much a turnkey operation – just put the key in the door, turn it, walk in and begin operating.

The franchisor usually derives profit from the initial upfront fee paid by the franchisee for access to their intellectual property, and then an ongoing fee, which can be based on turnover or some other determining factor. The franchisee also contributes to an advertising and marketing fund – as a percentage of monthly turnover.

The working relationship is strictly laid out in the franchise agreement. The franchisee must conduct business strictly in accordance with the system, as detailed in the policy and procedures manual. While many franchisees may regard this as the down side of this model of franchising, the quid pro quo is that the franchisee receives a much greater level of support than working under the Product/Trade Name franchise model.

The advantage of this model, particularly from the franchisor's point-of-view, is that standardisation, uniformity and consistency are key principles in the business philosophy. The franchisor maintains control of certain key business functions, while the franchisee is able to 'behave' like a big company, but with the budget of a small company. They get more bang for their bucks.

Other models

Due to the very nature of the business world, things are never cut and dried. Things are seldom straightforward and simple. Differing situations and business considerations have resulted in unique solutions being developed to suit particular requirements.

The world of franchising is no different. Consequently you may come across franchise arrangements that, in reality, are more like independent distribution agreements, commissioned agencies, joint ventures or a combination of some of these. And some franchisors operate a mixture consisting of company owned branches or dealerships, joint ventures and franchises. Who said business was boring?

"Remember that if you franchise a bakery, you're no longer in the bakery business; you're in the franchising business."

Brad Sugars

▌ So You Want To Buy A Franchise, Do You?

Did you know? ... _____

Colonel Sanders actively began franchising his chicken business in 1952 at the age of 65.

When he sold his interest in the US Company for $2m in 1964, he had more than 600 franchised outlets in the USA and Canada.

Today, there are more than 11,000 KFC stores in more than 80 countries. They serve eight million customers each day.

Next to owning your own home, owning your own business has got to be the one thing most people aspire to. Both are underpinned by that sense of freedom, of not being controlled by others, that is at the heart of our very own identity.

Being in control of your time, your effort and, hopefully, your income are very powerful driving forces. There is something about being self-employed that appeals to the vast majority of us, even though to most, it will sadly remain a dream.

Let's explore the notion of being SELF-EMPLOYED. What does it actually mean and what, if any, are the characteristics of the self-employed?

This is usually the first jump on the entrepreneurial ladder and for most, it's the only jump. In fact, most entrepreneurs never seem to get past this level of growth in their business.

The truth is you really can't call it a business; you've really got to call it a JOB.

What's more, this job is most probably one of the worst jobs in the world. I think it's put best by this quote, taken from one of my live seminars: "Most people thought they worked for an idiot BEFORE they started their own business."

I really don't think most people who start their own business know what they're getting themselves into. In fact, most look at it as something glamorous, exciting, and with such a sense of new found freedom they're fooled into believing wealth is just a few days, weeks or months away.

To become self-employed, what usually happens is one of two things...

EITHER ... you're unemployed and looking for a new job when one morning you have what I call a Blinding Flash of the Obvious.

"I know," you say, "I'll start my own business. Then no one will ever be able to fire me."

And with all of the planning of the team that built and sailed the Titanic you get started.

OR ... you're working for someone else and you keep thinking these three things to yourself:

"I can do a better job myself."

"How come they get ALL the money, when I do all the work?" and,

"If I owned this company, I'd be the boss, I'd make everyone else do the work, I'd play golf, relax, and I'd work a lot less."

Either way, there is one thing running through the mind of every single man or woman as they jump into the role of the Self-Employed Entrepreneur ...

"I'm going to be the boss ..."

And with that the race starts.

It's one of the biggest steps you'll ever take, and believe me, the most rewarding you'll ever choose, so if you're about to take it, that's great. Get ready to learn how to make it work for you ...

Almost an extension of the mindset challenges we've just looked at, most self-employed people's relationship with money needs to be examined.

As you may or may not know, the way you relate to money will determine your financial future. And, given you've only got one shot at this thing called life, let's make sure you give it the best shot you can.

A self-employed person has a very similar relationship to money as that of an employee. And we all know that as an employee you EARN money. What kind of word is EARN? It's a verb or DO'ing word.

With the self-employed, the word changes but the DO'ing-ness remains the same. They're still trading time for money. And their word in relation to bringing in money is now, MAKE.

They have to MAKE money in their business.

The dictionary definition of 'make' is: 'To bring into existence, especially by effort.'

So by definition, with this relationship to money you're still going to be working hard for every dollar you get. You're still trading time for money. Yes, you may be getting more dollars for each hour you work, but the see-saw effect of self-employment never lets you create financial freedom. More on that in a moment.

Whilst we're on definitions, here's the definition for 'Self': 'Person's nature, special qualities, one's own personality.'

And the definition for 'Employed': 'Give work to, usually for payment.'

Once again by definition you've positioned yourself in a place that from a true Entrepreneur's viewpoint is not only guaranteed to mean physical involvement in your money-making activities, but also that there's very little difference to being employed by someone else.

The only real difference is now you have the headaches of being both an employee and an employer.

Yet I want you to remember this: becoming self-employed is the first step on the ladder of financial freedom, and those who have taken it are usually far closer to becoming financially free than those who never do.

So, congratulations if you have, and congratulations in advance if you're about to …

Now it's time to think through some of the reasons people have for becoming self-employed. And they must be powerful ones, considering all the uncertainty and hard work most will be putting themselves through.

So what are they?

To my mind there are at least eight very powerful reasons for being self-employed. Reasons that, simply put, are a must if you're at all serious about getting yourself into the ranks of the RICH …

Employees have absolutely no true leverage; they're simply trading time for dollars. Keep this in mind.

When you're selling for yourself, there's no set hourly rate … you, through your skills, your level of work and your passion or determination, are able to determine your level of income. No one else can make that decision for a self-employed person. And, whilst that scares some, it feels great to many who take this step.

In fact, that level of self-control promised by the 'I did it my way' feeling is central to the decision most people make when becoming self-employed. Whilst being your own boss, and the ability to determine your own hours and income, are seen as the main reasons why anyone would choose to become self-employed, they are not the reasons I would give you to make this step.

So, what are my reasons for becoming self-employed?

Reason 1 … You'll have to learn about company structure and set-up. You'll probably also need to understand the difference between a holding company and a trading company. Why you should always have two companies rather than one: one to own the assets, the other to trade and make the on-going profits.

Reason 2 … You'll also need to learn accounting, bookkeeping and how to interact with your accountant. You may, for the first time in your life, get yourself an accountant.

Knowing where to look for the answers to your questions about the Balance Sheet, the Profit and Loss Statement, the Cashflow or any Budgets you do is a must if you're ever to aspire to bigger and better things.

Think of accounting as a background part of day-to-day business, it's like the engine room. Without it you may as well be playing sport and not keeping score.

Reason 3 ... Probably the most important two things you'll ever learn as a self-employed person (if you didn't already as an employee) is sales and marketing.

Becoming a great salesperson is a must if you're going to sell a lot. Sales means everything from face-to-face, over the phone, cold calling and even getting over any fear you may have of talking to people. Sales also means doing presentations to groups and selling to more than one person at a time.

It's easy to say, but becoming great at sales requires a lot of reading, learning and application. It may even take you a few years, if you've never done it before as an employee.

And marketing, well what can I say that hasn't already been said? Together with sales, it's the lifeblood of any business. A true Entrepreneur knows that, while cost reduction is important, bringing in the cashflow is by far the most important area for any company.

You can cut costs to post a profit, but you can only sell your way to prosperity. Whilst 'sales' is the ability to turn a lead into a sale, 'marketing' is the ability to generate prospects at a reasonable price. Read my books, *Instant Cashflow, Instant Leads, Instant Promotion, Instant Sales, Instant Repeat Business,* and *Cash, Customers, and Ads that Sell* to make sure you know the best marketing information there is.

Now, let's look at **Reason 4 ...** As a new business owner, you get the privilege of doing everything yourself, and one thing you really get to learn is the meaning of the words "Hard Work". You'll often complete 16 or 20-hour days, six or seven days a week. Not because there is just so much work to do, but because you're having fun, you're learning, growing and most of all, because you're working out how to design a business as you go along. Growing a business is like riding a bike: once you've done it a few times, it gets really easy.

Think of all this extra work as your entrepreneurial apprenticeship being done after hours.

Reason 5 ... One of the most important lessons every new business owner learns is Cost Reductions. As a self-employed person, you'll be forced to scrimp and save, to recycle, to borrow, to use old second-hand stuff and to do whatever it takes to get by.

Once again, whilst it's most important for a company to bring in money, lack of control over your costs is a certain death knock for a small business. Learning this 'tight' way of doing business is great; you'll need to remember it, especially as you get bigger.

Reason 6 ... for becoming self-employed is to simply make contacts. The more people network, the easier you'll find it to do business; any business. Or, to put it another way, join as many networking groups as you can, go to as many seminars as you can, to not only learn, but to get yourself out there meeting other business people.

In business, the old axiom of 'who you know' is extremely important, so learn to meet lots of people.

Reason 7 ... As a self-employed person, you'll also have to relearn the meaning of Responsibility and Accountability. Nowhere else is it as important to learn these virtues than as the boss of your own company. The 'buck' really does start and stop with you.

Far too often the world of the employee is littered with 'pass the buck' people. When these people start or buy their own businesses, it's almost certain that they'll fail. Only those with the passion and desire to lead a life of total ownership will ever succeed in their own business.

Of course, another great reason (**Reason 8**) for becoming self-employed is to make more money. Usually a good employee will make a whole lot more money as a self-employed business owner. This is not just because they're making more, but because of all the appropriate and legal tax deductions they can claim, the fact they pay tax only on their profits and not on their entire wage, and the fact that they get to pay tax later than an employee would.

To top it all off, people seem to work harder when they know the dollars are going into their own pocket and not someone else's.

And the **Ninth** most important reason is so you at least start to learn technology. Hopefully, like many others, you learnt these lessons at someone else's expense as an employee, but if not, prepare for a lot of learning and growth as you get your first company up and running at a profit.

Technology is here to stay and it's a painful business life for anyone who decides not to make it an integral part of his or her knowledge base.

To finish off … whilst most think the reasons for becoming self-employed are to take control and to be the boss, the exact opposite is true for the serious Entrepreneur.

Start your small business now, even if it's part-time, to gain the knowledge you'll need in a few years time when you're playing with big dollars and running your big business.

Now, before I forget …

Remember I mentioned a concept called the See-Saw of the self-employed?

As a self-employed person, your business life will feel just like a see-saw. While it's often true a self-employed person can make more per hour than they ever could as an employee, the challenge comes down to how many hours are actually used in the background.

You'll spend half your life chasing the work doing Marketing, Sales and Administration and then you'll have so much work to do you'll have to flip over and start doing the work…

Doing the work is one side of the see-saw and Sales and Marketing is the other.

Chase the work, do the work, chase the work, do the work, chase the work, do the work … and so on …

It's this see-saw that stops a self-employed person ever really getting ahead. Once again, you're still in a situation where there's no real leverage. You still need to DO the work.

It's also this see-saw that gets most self-employed people to make one of two decisions: to either give it up and go back and get a job, or to take the plunge, jump in the deep end of business, make the decision to grow their business and to hire team members.

You see, what you should be aiming at here is to grow your business.

The first step to doing this is to think about your vision. Understand that as long as you can only ever see yourself running a one-person business, you'll never be anything more.

You've got to build a vision of a big business, a business that needs to be big to achieve the vision you set. Maybe your vision is to change the world, to change your industry or to be the best in your industry. Whatever your vision, the bigger it is, the bigger your business needs to become to complete it.

Set a vision of what your business will be like when you've finished building it. You see, you have to plan it from the start so at some stage in the near future, your business will run without you. Plan for it from the beginning.

Whilst we're on change, one of the most important changes you'll need to make is to your identity. You'll have to stop thinking of yourself as a worker and start thinking of yourself as a business owner.

For example, you may need to stop thinking of yourself as a plumber and become the owner of a plumbing business – an entrepreneur who's currently building a plumbing business. Or, you may have to remember to stop telling people you're a hairdresser and start thinking of yourself as the owner of a growing hairdressing empire.

One other thing here, stop thinking of yourself or your business as being SMALL … calling yourself a small business is extremely limiting. You can be a growth business, a prototype business or even think of yourself as a big business. Don't just change your own identity; change the identity of your business as well.

I know this all seems overly simplistic, and it could even be just a mind game, but it's by far the most important step you need to take on your way to becoming a successful business owner. Set your vision as soon as you can.

Next step you need to take is to change your goals.

Set larger goals, much larger goals. Ask for more and then be prepared to get it. There's nothing worse than the limits you place upon yourself by setting small goals. Goals that may at the time seem a stretch in reality might just get you to work a little harder.

You see, when you set goals that are entirely massive compared with your current results, it challenges you to think entirely differently and to do things entirely differently. And that in itself is essentially what this growth process is all about.

So there you have it – a quick overview of what being self-employed is all about. Still convinced this is the route for you to take?

Congratulations, you've just taken one of the biggest and most important decisions you'll every make. Now all you still need to do is to decide HOW you'll get into business for yourself.

In the Introduction to this book, I outlined the three ways you can go about it. I also mentioned that there are compelling reasons for choosing the Franchise option, in preference to a stand-alone business. The most important of these is that many of the pitfalls of starting up in business have been removed. Someone else has already tested and measured all the variables for you. Everything has been set up ready to go. And although you'll feel like you're out there 'doing your own thing', you'll not be left to your own devices. You'll have a well-constructed safety net there to catch you if you fall. You'll be able to concentrate your efforts on doing what it takes to generate cashflow without having your mind and energy diverted to deal with 'housekeeping' or behind-the-scenes issues that do not directly influence the amount of business you attract.

Buying a franchise is a terrific way to get into business without the risks involved in starting one up for yourself from scratch. It is well known that the failure rate of businesses, especially during the establishment phase, is very high indeed. Statistics show that something like 40 out of every 100 business will fail within the first three years. The average failure rate of franchised businesses is less than six out of every 100 (2001 FANZ Survey of Franchising).

Isn't that interesting!

Being a franchisee could be thought of as something like a cross between being self-employed and being an employee. You have the best of both worlds. You get to enjoy freedom, to be your own boss and to run your own show, yet with the security offered by being an employee. That's the beauty of it.

But it has to be pointed out that franchising is certainly not a bed of roses. Like anything else in life, it has advantages as well as disadvantages and it is up to you to weigh up the pros and cons for yourself. We all have different views about what level of risk we should take in business – some people are comfortable with higher levels of risk-taking than others. It all depends on your own particular situation.

So what do you have to weigh up when deciding whether the franchise option is the route to take? What kind of factors should you evaluate according to your own business plans and ambitions?

Let's think about some of the **advantages** first.

The first advantage of buying a franchise is the training you receive. You don't have to be a specialist in the field before you go into business for yourself, as you would if you were to open up a business by yourself in that same field.

Then there's the security offered by the franchisor. You're not alone. You will be able to tap into a wealth of knowledge and experience to help you overcome any challenges you're going to be confronted with along the way. And the level of risk you'll be operating with will be significantly reduced.

You'll be able to start out in business under the umbrella of an already well-established brand name, image and reputation. This won't apply, of course, if the franchise system itself is brand new. In this case, you should expect to buy in at considerably lower prices because you will be taking a larger business risk.

You won't need as much working capital by buying a franchise because the system will already have been streamlined and you'll be benefiting from the system's bulk buying power.

Another valuable advantage lies in the systems you'll be buying. You won't have to spend time and money developing them for yourself. And if business premises are involved, all the legalities, council requirements, red tape and other bureaucratic requirements are taken care of.

National advertising and promotional campaigns are very expensive, but with a franchise, you'll get it all for a very small fee. This level of promotion is very powerful indeed, and extremely hard to quantify.

You also get the benefits associated with the franchisor's patents, trademarks, copyrights, trade secrets and their ongoing research and development campaigns (if applicable). Any new developments will be passed on to you at the earliest opportunity. This very often gives franchisees a real market advantage.

Ongoing market research is also usually shared with franchisees. You see, it's just as much in the franchisor's interest as it is in yours that you have a marketing edge.

Another advantage could be that you get to operate in an exclusive territory or sales area. Now this isn't always the case, but where it is, it can give you a greater share of the existing market.

And one final advantage that's well worth considering: finance. You see, banks have long recognised the advantages of franchise companies and have tailored financial packages for franchisees that are far more attractive than those commonly available to other business owners.

These positives need to be considered against the following general negatives:

Most franchisees will be operating under a set of rigid controls or operating requirements that form part of the Franchise Agreement. You will not be free to do exactly what you please. Performance levels, standards, and other constraints will apply. To thrive (and in actual fact, to even survive) you will need to develop good communication and relationship skills. You will need to get on well with your franchisor.

You need to factor in to your budgets the fact that you will be required to pay ongoing fees to your franchisor. These fees may be based on sales, turnover or they could be set at a particular amount.

Many prospective franchisees will also be at a disadvantage when it comes to trying to access the quality of the franchisor. How can you really go about this? Should you take their word for it or should you conduct your own searches? How do you verify their figures? How relevant are the stories they will tell you? You could ask existing franchisees, but how will you know who the most representative ones are? Every franchise system has its high-flyers, its mediocre performers and its battlers. And if the truth be known, every system also has a core of disgruntled franchisees – those that blame everything, but themselves, for their situation. The last thing you'd want is to make contact with one of these while carrying out your due diligence. Yet you probably wouldn't want to talk to a high-flyer either, as you'd probably walk away with unrealistic expectations. This is a very real problem to which there is no easy answer. You'll just have to do the best you can and trust your instincts.

Another negative factor concerns how you go about selling your franchise. You see, most franchise agreements will have strict conditions relating to who you can sell your business to. The prospective purchaser still needs to be acceptable to the franchisor and will have to pass the same tests or requirements as you did. So while this may not influence how you run your business, it nevertheless is a restriction that limits your freedom. You do not have the final say.

This 'loss in independence' can have another potentially harmful consequence, and it can, in the franchise system, lead to the franchisee becoming too reliant on the franchisor, even for day-to-day operational matters. The franchisee can, over time, become lulled into a sense of false security which will, if left unchecked, rob him/her of the entrepreneurial spirit that lead to the decision to buy the franchise in the first place. He/she could lose his/her spark or zest for business, which will end up being detrimental to the business in no time at all.

And finally, a huge disadvantage lies in the fact that if the franchisor should go belly up, so will you. You might be running your franchise according to plan, but if the majority of others don't, you could pay the ultimate price. And there's no denying the fact that there have been unscrupulous franchisors in the past, and there will probably continue to be in the future.

These are some of the factors you need to weigh up before taking the plunge and signing on the bottom line.

> "To succeed in franchising, it is imperative that you can work with the people within your system."
>
> **Brad Sugars**

▐ The Business Mindset

Did you know? ... _____

Gerry Harvey and Ian Norman first established the Norman Ross chain of stores in 1961 and sold the business in 1982.

In 1982 they started a new business, to be called Harvey Norman, with the opening of a store in Auburn, Sydney.

The company was floated in 1987.

Before you jump in and buy yourself a franchise, there's one very important question you need to ask yourself: "Do I have the mindset of an Entrepreneur?"

You see, whether you make it or not in business all comes down to one fundamental characteristic that you absolutely must have, and that's the mindset of a businessperson.

If you don't have that natural, inbuilt nose for business, you're going to struggle to run your own business. You need to constantly strive for profitability, which means you need to have a keen eye on the five main business areas that together influence whether your business will be profitable or not. These areas are what I call The Business Chassis.

Most people don't really understand business and, therefore, they work too hard. In fact, most business people work on the three areas of the chassis that refer to results, instead of the areas that can transform the business into a profit powerhouse. You'll see what I mean in a minute. First, let me explain the parts of the chassis. Think of it as the formula for success.

Your Number Of Leads

This is the total number of potential buyers that you contacted or that contacted you last year. It's also known as prospects, or potentials. Most business people confuse responses, or the number of potential buyers, with results. Just because the phone is ringing doesn't mean the cash register is. What's even more amazing is that very few businesses even know how many leads they get a week, let alone from each and every marketing campaign. It's great to get a lot of leads, but then you've got to remember your conversion rate.

Conversion Rate

This is the percentage of people who did buy as opposed to those who could have bought. For example, if you had ten people walk through your store today and you sold to only three of them, you'd have a conversion rate of three out of ten, or 30%. This has got to be a literal goldmine in almost every business I walk in to. You've already got them interested; now you've just got to get them over the line. When I ask the average business owner about their conversion rate, they take a stab in the dark and tell me that it's between 60 and 70%. Just for fun, I get them to measure it, and a couple of weeks later we find that it's more like 20 or 30%. Imagine how you would feel.

You should feel great; in fact you should be excited, because if you're getting by at 20 or 30%, imagine how your business would run at 60 or 70%. Remember, double your conversion rate and you've just doubled your turnover.

Your Number Of Customers

This is the number of different customers you deal with. You work it out by multiplying the total number of leads by the conversion rate. Remember, *it's not about getting more customers*; you can't change that number. It's about getting more leads and then improving your conversion rate. These are the variables that lead to the result.

Your Number Of Transactions

Some of your customers will buy from you weekly, others monthly, others on the odd occasion and others just once in their lifetime. What you want to know now is the average. Not your best and not your worst, but the average number of times your customers buy from you in a year. Once again, here's another goldmine; most business people never collect a database of their past customers, let alone write to them, or call them and ask them to come back.

Your Average $$$ Sale

Here's one variable that at least some business owners do measure. Once again, some might spend $5,000, some just $5, but the average is what you're after. Just a few dollars on each and every sale could be all it takes to calculate. Add up your total $ sales and divide it by the number of sales.

Your Turnover

This is another result. Multiply the total number of customers you dealt with, by the number of times they came back on average, and then by the average amount they spent with you each time. That's your turnover. Put simply, Customers x Transactions x Average $$$ Sale = Turnover. This is another area most business owners will know the answer too. Yet they most probably have no real idea how they got to it. Of course, you want more of it, but *you can't get more turnover*, what you can get is more transactions, and a higher average dollar sale with the total number of customers you deal with.

Your Margins

This is the percentage of each and every sale that's profit. In other words, if you sold something for $100 and $25 was profit, then you've got a 25% margin. Remember, this is after all costs have been taken out. It's potentially another little goldmine for you to tap into.

Your Profits

Another result that every business owner wants more of, not realising that *you can't get more profit.* What you can get is get greater margins on the turnover you've got.

And that's it.

The Business Chassis is the basic model that dictates the profit levels of every business on earth.

By simply breaking down your business and marketing efforts *(selling is married to marketing)* into these five areas and understanding how each affects the other, you're halfway there … and way ahead of 90% of businesses out there.

So this then is what The Business Chassis looks like:
(refer to opposite page)

LEADS
(prospects or potential customers)

X

CONVERSION RATE
(the difference between those that could have bought and those that did)

=

CUSTOMERS
(the number of different customers you deal with)

X

NUMBER OF TRANSACTIONS
(the average number of times each customer bought from you that year)

X

AVERAGE DOLLAR SALE PRICE
(the average price of the items you sell)

=

TOTAL TURNOVER
(the total revenue of the business)

X

MARGINS
(the percentage of each sale that's profit)

=

PROFIT
(something every business owner wants more of)

Does the thought of increasing your level of profitability send your pulse racing? Do you find the whole concept of increasing how much you make by tweaking the various variables in The Business Chassis fascinating? Has it already sent your mind into overdrive? Have you already identified a few things you just can't wait to try out? If the answer to these simple questions was in the affirmative, then you may have what it takes.

If, on the other hand, you are currently working for a boss, you still might have what it takes. But you do need to be aware that when you are your own boss, your entire approach to business will be very different to what it was when you were an employee. You see, you'll no longer instinctively reach for a new ream of paper when your photocopy machine runs empty. You'll think twice – or three times – before you raid your stationery cupboard. You'll most probably first check to see if you have any recycled paper you can use – paper that you have already printed on one side but decided not to use. You know the stuff; it's that paper you would previously have thrown into the bin. You will very soon begin to realise that, when you're running your own business, every cent you spend comes out of your own pocket. And this means potentially lower profits. You'll see things in a new light. You'll question everything.

Does this sound like you?

If you're still not sure, let's delve a little deeper into the mindset of an entrepreneur.

But first, let's quickly discuss the word entrepreneur. What exactly is an entrepreneur? Entrepreneur can be defined as a person who organises a business venture and assumes the risk for it. All entrepreneurs aren't the same. There are different types of entrepreneur. That should be obvious to you, but why exactly are they different?

The way I describe it is like this; they operate on five different levels. Let me now explain the way their mind's work at these levels. And I'll start off by explaining the mindset of an employee first, because this will help highlight very clearly to you whether you have the mindset of a businessperson or not.

The Entrepreneurial Mindset Of The Level Zero – The Employee

There are so many fundamental thought patterns that show up in a group of employees. Some are extremely rare and others are a part of almost every employee you meet.

I'm just going to examine their five biggest beliefs that relate directly to money, wealth, and becoming an entrepreneur. Remember, every thought pattern or belief that you have, in some way assists you and in others limits you. Something that may make you a great employee will truly limit you as an entrepreneur.

Friends invited me over for dinner recently. They had also invited some other friends of theirs. Several of them turned out to be serious employees.

They would ask questions like: "Who do you work for?" "How much do you earn?" But the one I liked most of all was: "What car do you drive?"

Now, I don't mean to be rude, but to some I will be. These people fell into the category I call 'LOOKING GOOD, GOING NOWHERE ...'

They would rather look rich, than be rich. Another way to describe their lives would be to say that they live them secondhand. They do everything to build an impression of themselves to the outside world, and when the outside world says it's true, they believe it - even though it's just an illusion they've created. A second-hand opinion.

So, often just changing a couple of simple thoughts or beliefs could dramatically affect not only their financial lives, but also their emotional lives.

With this in mind, let's find the essential beliefs that have them and other Level Zero Employees trapped in that little mouse's wheel - always running; yet standing still.

Firstly, the belief is that 'STUFF' is more important than WEALTH.

And, you know the 'STUFF' I'm alluding to. It's that dress you bought last week that you really didn't need. Those new Nike running shoes you bought because you liked the colours. The STUFF you want, the STUFF that chews up all your money, the STUFF that seems SO important when you're buying it ... the STUFF that rarely matters when you realise you're actually broke.

I'll be as blunt as I can ... spend your entire life buying STUFF and you'll end up with STUFF ALL.

Remember this; people should be first on your priority scale, money and wealth second, and STUFF - or things - a very distant third.

Now, don't get me wrong, I own LOTS of STUFF ... but it's in proportion ... I also have lots of investments, cash, businesses, properties and so on ... WEALTH pays for my stuff whether I get out of bed or not.

By the way, whenever you want to buy STUFF ... you should learn how to make it a tax deduction.

Keep your 'STUFF' in perspective. Sure, have it, but don't become obsessed with it.

Onto the second Level Zero belief we need to look at: Your income is representative of your wealth.

I think I've already beaten this one with a stick, but just in case I haven't made my case absolutely clear, let me go over it again.

Your income and your wealth are two entirely separate, and in most cases, non-related items. I've met people who make over a million dollars a year in salary, yet they are still poor because they spend more than that million on STUFF.

I've met a 22 year old young man who's never made more than $18,000 a year before tax and who has a net worth in excess of half a million dollars in his property portfolio.

Your income doesn't determine your wealth. It's what you do with your income that determines your wealth.

Remember, income does not equal wealth.

The third belief I want to examine and discard is this: Because I'm more intelligent, more skilled or more experienced, I have a higher chance of becoming wealthy.

Once again, I've met a lot of very poor professors and very rich high school drop-outs.

For some reason we've come to equate good grades, good training, or good skills as the key ingredient to success. This is especially so in the world of the Level Zero Employee.

An entrepreneur knows that courage, taking action and leadership are more important than scholastic intelligence.

In my world, my team of business coaches and I are continually working with people who 'thought they knew everything about business'. Remember this; nothing beats hard work, integrity, people skills, sales skills and the desire to take a risk or two to turn it all into reality.

This clearly brings us to the fourth (and by far the most challenging) belief most employees struggle with; the security of the steady pay cheque.

What's more secure ... a business with one customer who buys everything you produce, or a business with tens of thousands of customers who each buy a small portion of what you produce, and who keep coming back to buy more?

Of course it's not the one with a single customer. The JOB, with just one boss, even though it feels like it's more secure, is not.

One of the biggest challenges I have when working with Level Zero Employees is that they make their decisions based on fear - on what could go wrong - rather than on vision, trust, and on what can go right.

Fear, in almost all cases, is the one thing stopping people making the leap from Level Zero to Level 1 and beyond.

This introduces the reason for fear, or belief number five on our hit list: 'I don't know enough to start my own business'.

Jumping from Level Zero into the world of business requires a fundamental shift in thinking. It requires a shift from a thought process of fear to a thought process of trust.

Trust in yourself.

Trusting you'll learn along the way, trusting you'll make mistakes, but that you can recover. Trusting the only way to truly learn how to be an entrepreneur is to just get started.

Remember, fear of the unknown is natural. But, living a life without the courage to step through your fears is unnatural.

All greatness follows a leap of faith, a courageous step into the unknown, into a world of new things, new challenges and new possibilities.

Understand this; anyone can make the jump from Level Zero to Level 1. It takes courage, trust and self-belief. It also takes *Action.*

The Entrepreneurial Mindset Of The Level 1 – The Self-Employed

You see, while the emotional driving force behind most employees is security, those who step into the role of the self-employed are driven by another emotional factor.

This is the desire to be in CONTROL of their own life, and of their own destiny.

And, armed with this desire and marching to their theme song, Frank Sinatra's, 'I did it MY way' they're off to create something they never expected.

They're going to create a JOB.

A self-employed person starts out with just one employee; himself or herself. And that suits them fine; no one else to worry about, none of those other people who make all the mistakes, it's just them.

The self-employed person usually trusts no one other than themself to get the job done.

They'll say things like: "I am my business." Or, in their sales pitch: "You'll be dealing directly with me and I'm the owner of the business". Or, "If you want something done right, you've got to do it yourself." Or, "Everything is under my control so I know that it's done right."

Remember, most self-employed people started their own business because they thought they were so good at what they did, or so good at making what they sell, they mistakenly assumed they could run a business that sells what they make or do.

This mindset of being the eternally great employee was fantastic when you worked for someone else, but as you'll soon see, it's the fastest way to hard work, and often bankruptcy, as a business owner.

Starting a business where you are an expert at what the business does is usually the first and biggest mistake made by the majority of people going into business.

They start a business in which they know how to make what the business sells, instead of starting, or buying, a business in which they know how to sell what the business makes.

This is the start of the self-employed trap.

If you can do what the business does, and especially if you're the best at it, then it's almost a sure thing you're going to be trapped doing that work forever and a day.

Now, while the trap has already been set, it's this second factor that usually ensures every self-employed person falls into it.

Not only do they desire control, and think that no one is as good as they are, but ...**they don't have a VISION of 'doing' anything else.**

In general, their entire vision is limited by their previous training as a Level Zero Employee. They've never been trained that when you set up a company, you have to start with the end in mind.

You have to start it knowing that what you're doing is creating something that'll work without you. More about the specifics of this as we go on, but first, let's look at making your vision break-through.

What entrepreneurs know that most self-employed have yet to learn is how to envision in their mind and then put on paper what they see as the future of the business.

The self-employed are trapped by the limited 'doing' vision that is a part of being an employee. As an example, computer technicians who start their own businesses usually sees themselves servicing peoples' computers and would be extremely happy if they could get enough business to keep themselves, and only themselves, extremely busy.

In other words, most Level 1 Self-Employed people want to be BUSY. They seem to think that business is spelt – BUSYness.

Now don't get me wrong. By accident, some will break through this trap all on their own, BUT most are truly set to stay right here until they reach a point of frustration - a frustration that leads to more than 80% of Level 1 Self-Employed people calling it quits.

They say: "It's not worth all the trouble. I'm going back to get a job and work for someone else."

So, before you make the same mistake, let's examine this vision thing.

When you go into business you need to create a vision that not only sees the business working without you, but one that will inspire and enrol the people who'll be joining your team. You need to be able to see your business as more than just yourself.

You need to see it as a true business, and NOT just as a job for yourself.

You need to create a vision of YOU being more than just a worker in your own business - more than just a manager in your own business. You need to create a Vision of a business that works without you … in other words, an investment; your investment.

More about this as we get into the next few levels of entrepreneurs.

The Entrepreneurial Mindset Of The Level 2 - The Manager

Most people who get stuck at the Manager level are prone to a set of beliefs about business that is the only thing standing in the way of their success.

Firstly, let's deal with the total mistaken business belief 'Bigger is Better'. For some insane reason it's become a socially accepted belief that the bigger you grow your business the better it will be. Along the same lines it's thought by some, that the way to solve all your business woes is to just get bigger.

How wrong can two assumptions be! It's kind of like motivating idiots; they just do stupid things faster.

Growing bigger when you're running a business that demands you being there all day, every day, is just plain lunacy. If you found it hard to cope with the mistakes and errors when you dealt with 20 customers each day, what do you think you'll inherit with 200 customers per day?

I've seen so many companies grow themselves to death; it's not funny. Growing so fast, robbing Peter to pay Paul, and all the while their mistakes and lack of profitability is covered over by their rate of growth and the extra people they employ.

These companies seem to survive, although, no one really knows how or why. Many then fall into the trap of the second belief …More Employees means More Success …

Once again this is a completely crazy scenario. So much so I laugh when I hear someone bragging about how many people they employ. They seem to think because they pay a huge wages bill each month they must be more successful than the rest of us.

Not so. All this means is rather than turning to a better solution to run their business, they've turned to an older, outdated solution called 'hire more people'. If only they'd realised business has nothing to do with how many people you employ and everything to do with how much money you make.

Oh, that reminds me ... NOT ... More Revenue means More Success ...

Oh no, this is another beautiful example of ego overriding brain power, logic and common sense, just to name a few.

Now admittedly your total revenues can determine your company's value, but nowhere near the extent that profits can.

If only they'd realise bigger is not better and stop growing for the sake of growing, they might realise profit is the only score that really counts.

One last belief the Level 2 Managers seem to have found for themselves. They truly believe that ... 'Nobody's as Good as Me'.

And what's more, in most cases it's true.

Why? Not because the employees, or as I call them - team members, can't be good, but because the Manager is a bad leader.

In most cases, the employees have had bad training, bad goal setting, bad everything and most importantly, no-where near enough experience.

Managers hire people they can control rather than people they can lead.

I think it was Henry Ford who said: "The smartest people in the world hire people smarter than themselves."

However, the Manager seems to have this firm belief: 'If you want the job done right, you've got to do it yourself'.

All because they want to be the boss and feel super important.

Probably the biggest ego trip of all for Level 2 Managers is that of being the boss. Our Level 1 friends sang along with Frank Sinatra, yet our Level 2 buddies have no theme song ... just a firm desire to be Bruce Springsteen ... The Boss.

They seem to love the power of being in charge more than they love the profits, more than watching others succeed, more than seeing a manual task completed and much more than going home early and trusting other people to do a great job.

Now of course those still stuck at Level 2 will be reading this and feeling ready to kill me, or they will totally refute everything I've said, and with good reason (excuses) as to why their situation is different. And yes, it is different; but they now have the choice to change.

By the way, one last belief you'll have to remove if you really want to move and grow: The old 'I just can't get good people' belief.

I remember saying this to my Dad when I was 21. He replied very bluntly, as he so often did: "Brad, you're getting the people you deserve."

It took me quite some time to calm down and realise what he said was a simple truth. When I started running a great company I'd get great people, and when I became a great leader, I started running a great company.

I know this all seems so simple, but often the most profound ideas are the simplest. Become a great leader, you'll get great people and they'll run the business for you.

The Entrepreneurial Mindset Of The Level 3 – The Owner/Leader

Owner/Leaders experience a massive mindset shift when they first move up to this level. They operate on an entirely different level to the Manager.

Their relationship to the business is entirely different for a start. This brings with it a different way of doing things.

As an Owner/Leader, one of the first most important attributes you will have is that you receive passive income. You've reached the position where it doesn't matter whether you get out of bed or not each day. The business can carry on without you having to be there.

You see, you have progressed from working IN the business to working ON the business and now you can relax. This might take some getting used to, especially as you're so used to doing things yourself because nobody else could do it as well as you could.

As an Owner/Leader you're NOT a hands-on person. This means you'll take a more holistic view of the business. You'll be operating at the strategic level and concentrating on the big picture. Your focus is no longer on CASHFLOW (others do that now), but on PROFIT. The question you'll ask most often is: "Where's the Profit?"

The Entrepreneurial Mindset Of The Level 4 – The Investor

Because Level 4 is all about INVESTING, or MAKING MONEY WITH MONEY to create WEALTH, you'll be sufficiently removed from the day-to-day running of your business to concentrate on the task at hand.

Operating at this level, you'll want to keep things SIMPLE. Forget about setting up complicated business structures and reporting relationships. Avoid the temptation of empire building. Your immediate goal is the creation of wealth through buying and selling businesses. That's all. You can, of course, aim to buy and sell many businesses each year. Buy one at a rock bottom price, build it up, and then sell at a premium price. Use the proceeds from the sale, or some of them at least, to buy investment property and stocks. Read my book **Real Money, Real Estate** to find out more about winning the real estate game by establishing Property Wealth Wheels. Do this time and time again, using the knowledge and systems you've learnt before.

This brings me to another important concept; LEVERAGE. You'll be looking to exert as much leverage as you can in your business dealings at this level. If you are going to be building up businesses, chances are you will be using the same or very similar THINGS or SERVICES you will be buying from various suppliers. This is where you will be making use of bulk buying or the loyalty factor to get the best possible prices. You see, what you're ultimately aiming to achieve here is to acquire businesses as cheaply as possible, then to build them up into a saleable commodity that has real intrinsic value, through leverage, so other business owners will want to buy them.

Understand this: most people looking to buy a business want one that has already been built up by someone else. They want a going concern.

They want one that has been set up properly and is making a demonstrable profit. They want to be able to see that all the systems are in place and everything is running smoothly, just as much as they will want to examine the books and financial data.

It may seem obvious, but one of your basic goals when buying these businesses is to get a GOOD DEAL. It doesn't matter in the least whether you happen to like the business you're looking at, or whether it is making a good profit. The deal must be very attractive. It must make good business sense.

And never pay the full asking price – always aim to buy wholesale. If you think about it, why would you contribute towards someone else's profit if you are buying a struggling business – one that isn't doing well at all and about to go under? If it were thriving with good systems in place, then you wouldn't be looking at it in the first place, would you? There'd be little room for improvement and little chance of achieving a dramatically higher price for it when the time comes to sell it. And it wouldn't be contributing towards achieving your business goals and creating wealth.

By now, you'll be having a tremendous amount of fun, buying and selling businesses and building up your own personal wealth. Things will be starting to happen at different paces, different intensities and different levels. Unless you're careful, you could find yourself drawn back into the thick of things. You could become bogged down and unable to continue finding, buying and selling businesses. You'll realise that what you need is a PRESIDENT.

The Entrepreneurial Mindset Of The Level 5 - The True Entrepreneur

To get to this level, you've got to have learnt along the way. You have to have gathered knowledge. You now need to change the way you think. You see, you can't be rich if you don't think like a rich person does. It's that simple. Changing the way you think involves the following four-step process:

- Idealisation. Create your ideal world in your mind. Think big. Include everything you ever dreamed of.

- Visualisation. Picture that ideal world as if it were real. Do this twice each day, at 10am and again at 10pm, when you have some quiet time. Spend ten minutes each session thinking about your ideal world.

- Verbalisation. Talk about your ideal world as if it were real.

- Materialisation. Things will now start to happen, whether you like it or not. Your ideal world will begin to become a reality. Opportunities will present themselves, you will meet influential people and your dreams will begin to come true.

The true entrepreneur makes money by raising capital, or to put it another way, by using other people's money to make money.

If the true entrepreneur has a catch phrase, it would surely be this: "Not with my money, you don't."

The true entrepreneur is a visionary, a dreamer of what could be. The true entrepreneur is able to see clearly that which does not yet exist.

The true entrepreneur already has a passive income stream as well as physical assets. The true entrepreneur already has wealth. But what will be achieved at this level is becoming rich through the addition of paper assets.

One other thing: you've probably heard of Bulls and Bears. How does this relate to the true entrepreneur? It's all about mindset … Bulls bet the market is going up and Bears bet it is going down. But there's one other character I'd like to introduce to you, and that's the Pig. Pigs are those people who just have no idea what's going on. They take tips and bets on anything they can, which in reality is nothing more than the leftovers from the real investors. And bear in mind you make money a lot faster as a Bear. This is because the market usually drops really fast and climbs relatively slowly.

So there you have it, the business mindset in a nutshell. How do you shape up? Did you recognise yourself there at all? And did this excite you? If not, perhaps owning your own business isn't for you. If this is the case, then buying a franchise will not be for you either. You see, just because a business is a franchise doesn't mean it comes with some magic formula that will make owning and running it any different to any other business. Just because it comes complete with a set of tried and tested systems doesn't mean you don't have to have a head for business.

A franchise isn't a magic formula to make money. You still need to think like a businessperson thinks; otherwise you'll go to the wall as sure as the sun will rise tomorrow morning.

"I've never been afraid to try something new."

Gerry Harvey

▊ Buying A Franchise

Did you know? ... _____

That the average length of time that current franchise systems have been franchising in Australia is eight years.

_____

OK, so you've thought about it long and hard, considered all the pros and cons and come to the conclusion that franchising is the way to go. What do you do next? How do you go about finding a franchise that suits your needs and satisfies your longer-term goals?

Where do you start?

The first thing you need to do is to gather as much information as you can about the types of franchising opportunities that are available. To be successful as a business owner – in any line of business – you need to remember one very important thing: avoid buying a business that does what you used to do before you went into business. By this I mean if you are a qualified hairdresser, don't buy a hairdressing salon. If you do, you'll end up doing all the work. It's true. You'll do it because you know that no one you employ could do it better than you can.

This is one of the biggest traps business owners fall into. It traps them into working IN the business and not ON it. If they are the one doing all the work, who's going to be managing the business? Who will be doing the forward planning, the chasing after new business, the marketing campaigns and the management of team members? I'll tell you who – NOBODY, because you won't have the time. You might try to initially, but after a short while, you'll tire of the long hours you spend toiling away at what will soon become JUST ANOTHER JOB. You'll find you won't be able to pay yourself a salary because you'll be required to pay what you make to those who work for you. "Oh, it'll come right in a few months time," you'll tell yourself. "I'll consider it as an investment in my business

– then I'll draw enough to make up for it." Sound familiar? Heard other business owners say this? Of course you have. It's something they all say.

But I'll tell you something – it's all rubbish. Absolute garbage. If this is the approach you take, your business will never get off the ground. After a while, you'll either grow totally frustrated at having to slave away in your business for little or no reward, or you'll throw in the towel and go back to being an employee.

And here's another truism. This scenario will be all the more likely if it is your first business venture. That's one reason why I recommend people buy their first few businesses as a franchise because many of these pitfalls have been taken care of. They will, by virtue of their franchise agreement and operations manual, have to spend time working ON the business even though they might, due to the nature of the franchise, have to work IN it at the same time.

Even though you might have to DO the work if you buy a one-man-band franchise (like lawn mowing or dog washing), you'll avoid many of the pitfalls mentioned above because the franchisor will provide you with thorough and comprehensive training. And this will include how to work IN the business as well as how to work ON it. And they should have systems in place to ensure you don't stray into the IN area too much. If they don't, be wary.

So where is the best place to find information about which franchises are for sale? The easiest place to start is by looking through the Businesses For Sale section of your local metropolitan newspaper. There you'll find display ads for major franchises that are for sale at that time. These ads are far larger than normal classified ads and carry much more information. You need to bear in mind that, at this stage, you are still doing your homework and hunting for information of a more general nature. This is precisely what you'll find in display ads.

You'll find information about the franchise system itself, its size and possibly how long it has been in operation, what they provide, the locality of stores or areas that are for sale, and a bit about the lifestyle you'll have by buying one. The price will seldom be mentioned at this stage. There will always be some kind of invitation to make contact. You see, the aim of these ads is to entice you to find out more.

Isn't that the aim of all ads, you might ask? Well, no, not exactly. Traditional ads aim at getting you to buy something, either by visiting the store or by taking some other form of action. They usually try to persuade you why you should buy that particular product and not the one from the competitor. Price and benefits are major factors in doing this.

With franchising it's different. Sure the master franchisor wants to sell franchises. It is, after all, the ongoing sale of franchises that keeps them in business. But the difference lies in the fact that they don't want to sell a franchise to just anyone. Having the right amount of dollars isn't enough. They need to ensure you meet other important criteria, such as the right attitude and temperament, the right approach to business and sufficient working capital to see you through start-up. They will want to ensure that you'll fit comfortably within the franchise network and that you will be suitable for that type of business. They will also want to make sure that you will be comfortable working within a system and not branching off doing your own thing.

You should also look at the Business Classifieds for information, however fleeting, about franchises that are on the market. Here again, don't expect to find out too much – it's just the starting point. But it's in the classifieds that you'll often come across bargain buys. You see, people are only human and they make mistakes. Very often someone buys a franchise only to find out it's not for them. They need to off load the franchise and are prepared to let it go cheaper just to get out. People also become ill or suffer other tragedies that necessitate the sale of their business. If you come across one of these, you'll still need to go through a vetting and acceptance process with the franchisor.

Another good source of franchises for sale is the business press. These are specialist magazines that are available at all leading newsagents. Some focus only on businesses for sale, while others focus on business opportunities. There are even specialist franchise magazines, which I recommend you read in any event, because in them you'll be able to quickly assess what the franchise industry is all about and what it's like running many of the more popular franchises. They run in-depth feature articles on many aspects of franchising on a regular basis as well as columns dedicated to answering many of the more common questions and challenges franchise operators have.

These days the Internet plays an important role in our lives and it is here you'll come across lots of important information about franchise systems, what they involve and how to enquire further. Always check out the site of the major Franchise Association in your country as you'll find a wealth of unbiased information about different franchise companies. You'll also come across their franchise sites, many of which are linked to the Associations' pages. Check out http://www.franchise.org.nz and http://www.fca.com.au

These organisations will also be able to supply you with material about what you need to think about when buying a franchise. Read it and digest it.

Then begin narrowing down your search for a suitable franchise by honing in on a selection of systems that appear at first glance to meet your requirements. Obviously you will, at this stage, be making your selection based on what can only be called superficial information, but at least you will be narrowing down the field. You will, be able to fairly easily eliminate much on offer just by reading about the type of work that will be involved. For instance, if you see yourself running a retail outlet of some description, you'd be able to flick lawn-mowing services, cleaning franchises, antenna installation businesses and business service franchises. Similarly, if you didn't have the better part of a half-million dollars or more to spend, you wouldn't be bothering with fast food outlets or clothing stores.

Once you've done that, the next thing to do is to start gathering more detailed information about them. Begin by checking out their web sites, visiting their stores or premises (if applicable) and looking at their consumer ads. Aim to get an idea of how the franchisees operate, what they charge and what sort of service they promise. Talk to customers to gauge public impressions. Try and find out if the franchisor has been involved in any legal issues with franchisees. Your local newspaper office is a good place to start. Their librarian might be able to do a search for you.

Once you've gone through this exercise, you'll probably be able to narrow your selection down even further. You might have decided to scrub one or two from the list.

Now it's time to start making contact.

Ring up the contact numbers listed in their ads, and request more information. It's quite likely at this stage that you'll be sent some more information, some of which may be in greater detail than you already have. You might even be asked to fill out some paperwork, which must be returned before you can proceed any further.

By now you will have a very good idea of what system you want to pursue. Your first fact-to-face meeting will not be far away.

This meeting will be a crucial part of your selection process because it will tell you a lot. And here I'm talking about those less obvious, but equally important, factors that are so important when going into business. Things like the corporate culture, the level of confidence and commitment those at management level have in their business, and whether you feel you'll fit in and get along with those who will be your superiors.

You should now be in a position to run with just one of your original selection of systems. You should be feeling comfortable within yourself about what you have gleaned so far and you should be feeling excited at the prospect that very soon you could be running your own business.

It's now time to start the official application process. This will most probably be a fairly lengthy and involved process, and for good reason. You see, you will be being assessed as much as you will be assessing the franchise system. And remember, it's all for your own good. Most franchisors are only to well aware of the fact that too many franchisee failures ultimately damages their business. Word soon gets out and causes not only new prospects to become ultra wary, but existing franchisees become nervous too and begin talking among themselves. This can spiral out of hand very quickly, even if there is no foundation to their fears. And lastly, a thorough assessment of your own suitability for the business is in your own interest, because mismatches are very costly.

This is the time to re-evaluate your financial situation. Make absolutely sure you have sufficient capital at your disposal. You will, by now, have a pretty good idea of what this franchise is going to cost you as the details will have been discussed at some length during one of your many face-to-face meetings.

Discuss your options with your bank manager, accountant or any other financial advisers you might have. And be aware that some franchise systems will have vendor finance on offer while others will want to ensure you have ALL the funds readily available – they will not allow you to borrow, even from your own family. Weigh up your options carefully – even if you are offered vendor finance. You see, if the franchisor lends you some or all of the money required to buy into the business, what would happen to you if they were to get into financial difficulty? Creditors would make a beeline to you and demand you repaid the cash.

And remember you'll need to ensure you have sufficient working capital at your disposal. This is in addition to the purchase price of the franchise. To be on the safe side, work on not earning an income for up to three months. Make sure you budget for your normal living expenses like repaying your mortgage or rent, rates, car expenses, food, clothing, schooling, telephone, entertainment and electricity. You might want to tighten the belt a little during this period, and that's fine; just be sure to include everything in your budget. And don't forget to include any business-related expenses like royalties, franchise fees, team member salaries, stock, rent, telephone, equipment leases and insurance. Not all of these may apply to you, but think laterally and draw up an initial start-up phase budget.

Of course, the sooner you are able to get your cashflow running, the better. And having an onerous budget hanging over your head is also a great motivator to make things start happening in your new business sooner rather than later.

One final bit of advice here; keep scrupulous records of absolutely everything. You see, not only will this come in real handy when you get around to filing your tax return, but you can't manage what you can't measure.

Once you've satisfied yourself that you have access to sufficient capital to at least see you through until you've established your business – when it should be bringing in enough money to cover all the running costs – you need to turn your attention to the Disclosure Documents you will have been given by the franchisor.

In Australia, franchisors are required to provide prospective franchisees with a disclosure document. This is a requirement of the mandatory Franchising Code of Practice. The Code was recently amended to extend the purpose of the Disclosure Document, which is now not only to give a prospective franchisee information to help them make a reasonably informed decision about the franchise, but also to give them current information that is essential to running the franchised business. Furthermore, there is now a new requirement for the franchisor to continue to maintain a current Disclosure Document for a year after they have ceased entering into franchise agreements.

In New Zealand, because the self-regulatory Code of Practice only applies to members of the Association, only franchisors that are members need to produce a detailed Disclosure Document. You see, there is no specific legislation governing franchising in New Zealand, but that doesn't mean franchising there is overly risky. You will still be covered by the normal consumer protection measures they have in place, as well as that country's commercial laws. So, deal with members if you want extra peace of mind. The Disclosure Document covers a wide range of areas including key details of the franchise, the franchisor's financial track record, details of all payments required, information on any litigation between the franchisor and franchisees, and clarification of any projections made. This must be provided to you at least 14 days prior to you being required to sign the agreement to enable you to have sufficient time to seek independent legal and financial advice. The Code also provides for a seven-day cooling off period and sets out a disputes procedure for resolving problems between franchisors and franchisees.

Once you have these documents, read through them thoroughly a few times. Try and understand as much as you can, and place this information in context, bearing in mind your own personal situation. Is there anything that can be 'read between the lines', and that can throw more light on the proposition? Is there anything there that, when added to other information you have collected, produces a different perspective on things?

Once you have digested all the information contained in the disclosure document, it's time to consult the experts. Make appointments to see an accountant and lawyer who are fully conversant with franchise matters. If your accountant is only a generalist who isn't too clued up about franchising, find one who is. There are many that specialise in this field.

If everything still stacks up after you have been given professional advice, and if you still feel that fire burning in your belly, then it's time to move on to the final step – the signing of the agreements. And don't forget you still have the protection of the cooling off period. Use this time constructively. Go through all your facts and figures once more. Check everything again to ensure you haven't overlooked anything. Has your situation changed in any way since you first began seriously investigating buying the franchise? Have any external factors changed? What about the state of the economy or the official bank rates? Consider every little factor, no matter how insignificant it may seem at first. Ask yourself 'what if' questions. What if you should become ill and hospitalised? What if your car was stolen? What if your house were to burn down? What if your partner should suddenly leave you? How would you cope?

Use this cooling off period wisely. After all, it is there for your own protection. It is a final way out for you should something suddenly change.

Of course, there may be other things you need to consider when buying a franchise. You might need to thoroughly investigate different factors depending on the type of franchise you are after. For instance, if you were chasing a petrol service station deal, you probably would want to look very carefully into the demographics of the area in which the proposed site is situated. Passing traffic, convenience, and local consumer trends and statistics would probably be some of the areas you'd want to look closely at. Retail stores in major shopping centres also have particular considerations like requirements regarding periodic shopfront refits and extended trading hours. What affects do they have on your cashflow predictions?

Brad's Top Tips For Buying A Franchise

- Ask yourself this: "Why am I looking at a business?" Am I looking to just buy myself a job, or do I have the entrepreneurial spirit that running my own business requires? If the thought of buying and running your own business paralyses you with fear, you need to question whether this is the right option for you. You see, most franchisees that fail do so because they are not suited to the system, and not the other way around. Many of them don't have the entrepreneurial mindset to run a business; they still have the mindset of an employee.

- If you could create the perfect business, what would that business be? Then begin looking for franchises that match the general idea you came up with. You see, you must enjoy what you end up doing. You'll find you'll be faced with a huge variety of possibilities from which to choose. Now choice is a good thing, but too much choice can also be bad in that it can cause you to procrastinate. Let me illustrate it this way: there may be lots of money to be made from running a dog grooming franchise, but if you can't stand animals, it wouldn't be the right thing for you. Sure you'll make money, but ... you need to be clear on what you want.

- Do your due diligence and speak to a few successful franchisees as well as some who are battling. Ask them these questions: "Why did you get into this business in the first place?" "What have been your greatest challenges and how did you overcome them?" "If you were given the chance again, would you reinvest in the business?" "What suggestions would you have for prospective buyers?" Then ask the franchisor these same questions and see if the answers match. Try to determine what their mindsets are and compare them to yours. But don't be put off by those that are struggling, if they are in the minority. If they are in the majority, look for another opportunity.

- Develop a business plan and ask some franchisees if they think it's achievable.

- Make sure you go through the legals thoroughly. Spend money consulting with a suitably qualified franchise lawyer. Understand exactly what is expected of you and what the franchisor will do for you. Contact the Law Society and ask them to recommend lawyers with good franchise experience. You see, if you go with an ordinary lawyer, you'll end up paying for hour upon hour of research time required for that lawyer to become suitably acquainted with franchise matters. So spend the extra upfront and hire a lawyer with franchise experience; it will be far cheaper in the long run. And don't be afraid to 'interview' a short list of lawyers before you settle on one.

- Get a suitably qualified accountant before you take the plunge and sign for the purchase of a franchise. They will help you to structure your future business so that you get maximum tax and financial benefit. Here again, choose one that has franchise experience – and interview them before you choose one.

- Look for a franchise system that meets your needs today as well as in five years time. Try to ascertain whether it will grow with you in time. Ask yourself whether it will be viable to branch your franchise out into a business of its own, if that's what you want in the medium to longer term. You see, you might do fine from a lawn mowing franchise for the first year or so, but should you want to operate another franchise in an adjacent territory, you might find you end up doing all the support work, the maintenance and marketing for your second franchise, resulting in lower returns from your initial business and a much greater workload. Some franchises are built to develop into bigger, self-sustaining businesses, allowing you to progress to the point where you can receive a passive income. So check this out to see if the franchise fits with your longer-term aspirations.

- Seek the advice of those who know you best – your family and friends. Ask them if they think you'll succeed, then ask them why. This will help you avoid all the emotional stuff that so often gets in the way of making a good, sound decision.

- Ensure you have the full support of your family, especially if this is your first business venture. Running a franchise will affect your entire family and they will all have to make adjustments. If you're keen on a retail-type business, you'll probably find you won't have another weekend at home again, which can take some getting used to, especially if you came from the corporate world.

- If at all possible, try to arrange it so you can spend a day with a franchisee. This will give you a better idea of what the day in the life of an average franchisee is like. It'll give you a very good feel for what running the franchise will be like.

- Document everything that is said outside of the agreement. Get as much as you can in writing. You see, franchising is all about relationships, but if you've been promised something that isn't explicitly stated in the agreement, you could end up being very disappointed if the person who made the promise should leave. So get it in writing.

"The Number One business rule is PROFIT IS KING. The success of your business has nothing whatsoever to do with how much revenue it makes or how many people you employ. And it also has nothing to do with what market share it enjoys. It's all about profit."

Brad Sugars

▌ Selling A Franchise

Did you know? ... _____

VIP Lawnmowing Services started in 1972 and was the first company to franchise lawnmowing in Australia.

VIP now also offers franchise opportunities in home and commercial cleaning as well as window cleaning and mobile car washing and detailing.

Like everything in life, there comes a time when it's appropriate to move on. Nothing lasts forever, as they say. The same is true in business.

There could be a variety of reasons for wanting to move on – for wanting to sell your business. It could be that you have achieved your business goals with this particular business or it could be that a new, more lucrative, opportunity has presented itself. It could also be that you want to move to another city but can't move the business. It could be that you have become tired or bored with the business and can't give it the attention it needs to prosper. Or it could simply be that you just aren't making a success of it, and don't know what to do to maximise its earning potential. Perhaps you've realised buying the business was a mistake in the first place and you should never have bought it. Illness and family problems may dictate that you just can't keep going with it and it must be sold.

Every different reason brings with it a different level of MOTIVATION for selling. And it is this level of motivation that will ultimately dictate what price you are finally able to achieve. You see, if you are desperate and just have to get rid of it at all costs, then chances are astute business buyers will pick up on that and bargain accordingly. If you are in no particular rush and the business is doing fine, then you will probably be willing to sit and wait until you get your price.

You need to be aware of what signals you'll be giving out during the sales process. Think carefully here and don't act on impulse. Plan carefully because, whether you want to believe it or not, your actions will be seen by the market as your next move in this game we call business. Remember that; it's just a game. And games must be fun. So don't get too carried away, making things overly serious for yourself. Now I know selling a business is serious stuff, but don't stress out too much, plan your next few moves as if they were part of a game and you'll find you'll begin sending out positive signals that will be taken more seriously by the market. This will be to your benefit.

Selling a business will generally be one of the biggest decisions you'll ever make. And it will usually be one of the most important. This is because the amount you receive from its sale will generally form a large part of your wealth creation strategy or plans. Your future may depend on its outcome. Your financial viability might depend on it.

So let's spend some time considering the sale of your franchise from this larger financial perspective before getting down to the finer details.

The Big Picture

Understand that to be RICH you need to have two things that will allow you to produce the third desired outcome. You need a rather large CASHFLOW as well as a solid physical ASSET base. These two things combined allow you to create the third part of becoming RICH, and that's PAPER ASSETS.

Now, I know most people would be happy with being just WEALTHY … you know, lots of PASSIVE income and lots of physical ASSETS. That's fine. And it's easily achievable by buying, building and selling businesses.

But remember, the only reason you start a business is to sell it.

Generally speaking, you won't become RICH by owning just one company – you need to buy, build and sell businesses a few times over. A good strategy is to hang onto your first business for its passive income stream while you acquire and build up your next business. You will be able to do this because you should be aiming at getting your first business to run without you. This is important because it will allow you the time to devote to finding and building your next business. And expect to consider between 50 to 100 businesses before you settle on the next one.

When it comes time to sell your business, you'll need to be a good negotiator. You'll also need to be a good salesperson, but more on that in a while.

You're going to be aiming to get a far higher price for it than anyone else might if they were selling it simply because you'll have finished building it. The buyer just has to move in and start trading. Everything has been built up already. You'll have established the business in your area, it will have a strong and loyal client base and it will have impressive trading figures. In short, it will present well.

First Things First

The first thing you need to do is to go through your franchise agreement to find out what constraints or limitations you have when selling. Each system is different, and some will set out the price you have to sell for. Others will leave that up to you.

So, what price should you sell for? Are there any broad guidelines that you should follow? Yes, most definitely. Here's what I suggest.

If your franchise it trading well, then set a price based on two and a half to three times its annual turnover. So, for example, if your turnover is $100,000 a year, then set the price somewhere between $250,000 and $300,000. And then add some. If your franchise is losing money, set the price at replacement value. The aim of the game is to get a very good price for your finished business. After all, not only is this now the way you will be making money, but the buyer will be benefiting from all your knowledge, hard work, foresight and risk-taking.

When you think about it, you are selling your dream, right? What's more, you are not just selling a business, you are selling one that actually WORKS – the marketing works, the systems work, the people work – everything works to create the results. This is all guaranteed because you have built a definable relationship here. You will be able to show exactly what is happening in the business – who your customers are, how many times they buy from you, and what the average dollar spend is.

Also, negotiations always begin from the price. Buyers have to start somewhere. They will evaluate your business against the asking price and negotiate from there. Ask too low, and they will still negotiate down from that low price. Remember this; buyers decide based on price, not value.

The next thing you need to do is to consult your franchisor. This is vitally important because, not only do they usually have the right of first refusal, they also need to agree to the eventual purchaser. They may also have a procedure in place that you need to follow. And remember, too, that the franchisor usually has to be consulted every time you alter your selling price because they will, once again, have the right of first refusal.

Once you've taken care of these formalities, it's time to think about advertising your business for sale, using the best medium according to your individual situation. If you need help, call an *Action* Business Coach – they are specialists and can help you design an ad that works. Then it's just a matter of waiting for prospective buyers to make contact.

They'll want to see your operation, and they'll want to go through your books and talk about future potential. They'll then make an offer and expect to negotiate.

At this point, I'd like to remind you about the only reason you got started in the first place. You want to ultimately build up a passive income stream that will give you the ability to become self-sufficient; to become wealthy – to become rich. You have to think of yourself as a Business Trader, not just a Business Builder. Got it? You should be aiming to Buy, Build and Sell, and NOT to Buy, Build and Hold.

There may well be times when you decide to hold on to a business for a while, and that's fine.

I mentioned earlier that when you sell, you'll be aiming at achieving a higher price for it because you'll have finished building it. What do I mean by that? Well, you've finished building the business when you have achieved your vision for it. When it operates or functions as you originally dreamed it would when you first bought. Basically it is finished when all the systems are in place and operating as designed, allowing the business to run WITHOUT you. And there are very good reasons for finishing a business. Firstly, you will get a high price for it when you sell. Secondly, because it's now a finished business you can sell it through a broker, who will attract buyers with larger budgets. And thirdly, because the business is producing a passive income stream, you won't be under any pressure to sell. You'll have the luxury of holding it until you get your price.

Some of the things I set up as goals when I start building the business are the following:

- I want to know what my turnover will be on the day I finish building it.

- I want to know what my profit will be on the day I finish building it.

- I want to know what the date will be when I will finish building the business.

- I want to know what the sale price will be on the day I finish building it.

Your business will now be worth considerably more than when you first bought it. You will be aiming to get what it's worth – a very different scenario to when you were considering buying it in the first place.

Understand this: because the profit was built into the BUYING price, not the selling price, you'll be holding out for your price. That's the beauty of it. You will be able to afford to sit tight until the right deal comes along. The business will be running along very nicely without you needing to be there. You can then spend your time sifting through likely businesses to buy next.

Remember, my definition of a business. A business is a commercial, profitable enterprise that works without you.

So when is it you can walk away from your business? You can walk away from it as soon as all the systems are up and running and working as they should, and you have a fully trained team in place. The business will now be running itself. If it doesn't, or if snags occur, then you will need to look at fine-tuning some of the systems. Talk to your franchisor as there may be systems in place to help you do this. You see, franchise systems need to be dynamic; they also need to change with the times. This in itself is a good thing, because it will be testing your systems and people in real-time situations. Once you've ironed out all the teething problems, you should have a fool-proof business.

Businesses that run themselves will be attractive to investors precisely because they don't want to become tied down running the show in the first place. That's why they call themselves investors and not sole operators or things like that. The fact that you have developed the business to the point where it can run itself will be very appealing to the investor.

However, it is possible for a buyer to come along who intends running the business himself or herself. I call this selling to a technician. These buyers are looking to buy themselves a job, and that's fine if that's what they want.

Vendor Finance

With these buyers, if they are the only ones you get, be prepared to think about offering vendor finance, if your franchisor allows it. Your franchisor may also have the facility available for approved buyers. It may just make the difference between making a sale at a very good price, or hoping for a sale and not being sure.

What is vendor financing all about? Vendor finance can be very useful, particularly so if you are asking for a high price. In many instances, a buyer may not have ready access to a very large amount of money, but he or she might still be the perfect buyer for your business. And it might also be that, for whatever reason, the banks may not be a viable option for them.

Vendor financing often allows for a fast sale, as there are no lengthy delays while the traditional lenders study the finance application in detail.

Very often this is the only way for you to get your price. Buyers may well consider vendor finance as attractive because there may be no interest charges built in. You might offer a straight deal involving a set number of monthly repayments until the purchase price has been met.

Vendor finance also means there may be no capital gains to be taken into account. And the terms of the deal might ensure you keep an income stream from the business flowing that much longer. If the worst came to the worse, you could even state in the contract that, should things not run according to plan, you would get your business back. You would then have earned the monthly repayments along the way as well.

The Most Overlooked Target Market

When selling your franchise, don't forget another very important target market; your existing team (generally know as a management buyout) and employees with a payout. Let's look at them now in a little more detail.

Management buyouts are becoming an increasingly popular way of selling finished businesses. People running and working in a business often see ways of doing things better and of making improvements, if only the company were theirs.

Many also dream of owning their own business some day, and buying out the business that currently employs them means they don't have to leave and get involved with the unknown. They have always wanted to be the boss, and this could be the chance they have been waiting for. There is security in the familiar. Others could fear losing their job if someone else buys the business and appoints their own management team to run it. A management buyout could be a way of ensuring job security.

The question you have to ask yourself as a seller in this situation is can they raise the money?

If the business has been built and run properly, it will be producing good profits. Banks might be willing to finance a management buyout, particularly if the bank in question is the business's bank and therefore has a long relationship with it.

Vendor Finance is also an option to consider here.

I reckon the best buyer in the world has got to be an employee with a payout. It might be that one of your team members has received a large insurance payout or a retrenchment payout from a previous employer. By buying the business, it could allow them to just keep on doing things the way they always have. It offers safety and security. And by working in the business themselves they could save having to pay someone else a wage.

So don't overlook these two useful categories.

The Characteristics Of A Good Salesperson

Now let's look at another very important aspect that will have an impact on the eventual price you achieve from the sale of your business – your ability to sell.

That's right, there's no getting away from it; you have to be a good salesperson.

One of the common characteristics of all good salespeople is training. They train continuously. And they keep training. They do this for a number of very good reasons. Firstly, they want to keep up-to-date with the latest trends and techniques. And in today's fast-changing world, this can be a bit of a challenge. Secondly, they want to keep motivated. They want their energy levels replenished on a regular basis. One of the best ways of doing this is to rub shoulders with successful salespeople on a regular basis. You see, one of the powerful benefits of doing this is to hear from them what works and what doesn't. It also helps keep you focused on the bigger picture, on what is achievable and on how you can lift your game by emulating the best in the business. So look out for a sales course and enrol. You won't regret it.

To be successful in selling your business, you need to have strong beliefs. You need to have something you believe to be true. But more particularly, you need to hold a strong set of beliefs about your business, your potential buyers and the benefits your business will have for them.

You need to understand that, when a buyer is making up their mind whether to buy or not, the decision will be based on a mixture of fact and emotion. This is due to our human nature. We can't get away from it. But the important thing you need to know, when faced with a buyer in this situation, is what percentage of the decision will be based on fact, and what percentage on emotion. If you knew that, you'd be in a far better position to help with the process. Of course, this varies according to the type of business being considered, but on average, the decision is a mix of 20% logic and 80% emotion. How powerful is this to know?

To be successful at selling, you also need to hold strong beliefs about money. What does it mean to you and what role does it play as a motivator? It's pretty important to most salespeople, because their very remuneration package usually hinges on their performance. The more successful they are at selling, the more they earn – it's as simple as that.

Money seems to feature prominently in the life of a salesperson. And so it should. But what is money?

Let me give you my view.

Money is an idea backed by confidence.

Different, huh? That's right. To succeed out there, you need to see things differently. If you don't, you'll be no different from the rest. Understand this: if you see things just as everyone else does, you'll get the same results as they do. And we all know most salespeople don't make a fabulous living.

So let me run this past you once more. **Money is an idea backed by confidence**. Now here's another thing that may come as something of a surprise: the sales process actually starts with YOU. Long before you have a prospect to convert into a customer, and long before you are at the stage of selling your business to a prospect, you only have an idea. You have the idea that you'd like to sell your business to someone. Of course, you have this idea because it's what you want to do. You have already decided to sell your business for whatever reason. But you don't only have an idea. You have something more. You have confidence. That's right. Because you are a confident salesperson, you have confidence in your ability to sell. At this stage, you might not know who you will be selling to, but you'll probably have a vague idea. For instance, if your business is a panel beating shop, you're probably looking for someone in the trade or someone who already owns a similar business and who is looking at expanding. Now when you combine the idea with the confidence, the end result is money. The money will follow. Get it?

Now if you see money as I do, the way you set out to get it is by harnessing the power of the following four words: Attention, Interest, Desire, and *Action*.

You need to focus your attention on your goals. You then need to have a strong interest in achieving these goals. Mix this with a strong desire to achieve, and you'll be spurred into *Action*. You'll rise to the occasion and perform.

Every salesperson needs to be a good communicator to succeed. Communication is the lifeblood of business, and when it comes to sales, it's vital. It has a direct relationship with sales. You see, the better you are at communicating, the better your sales results will be. You can almost measure the one with the other. Actually one could be thought of as a barometer for the other. Let me put it another way. True communication is the response you get. So if you're not getting the response you want, you're not communicating properly.

Let's look at this in more detail. Communication, as far as sales is concerned, isn't confined to the words alone. It's far broader than that. In fact, when it comes to communicating, the salesperson has three tools at his disposal; words, voice and body language. And we use them all simultaneously. The interesting thing, as far as communication in the sales process is concerned, is that words account for only 7% of the eventual outcome, the voice is more significant at 38%, but by far the most important tool is body language, which weighs in at 55%.

Have a good look at these figures.

Remember what I said about your ideas and your confidence? Understand how they influence your body language, and you'll begin to grasp the importance of this in the sales process.

I'm now going to introduce another concept that has to do with communication in the broad sense. It's called Neuro-Linguistic Programming, or NLP for short. NLP is a model of human behaviour and communication that draws from the knowledge of psychodynamics and behavioural theories. It is concerned with the identification of both conscious and unconscious patterns in communication and behaviour and how they interact in the process of change.

So what does this mean as far as sales are concerned?

If we can understand the three key components of NLP, we can become better communicators. These are:

- Rapport and communication.

- Gathering information.

- Change strategies and interventions.

Rapport and communication covers areas such as language-representational systems, eye-accessing movements, verbal and nonverbal pacing and leading, communication translation skills, and representational system overlapping. These may sound terribly complicated, but the general idea is quite straightforward. If you want to go into them in more detail, there are many excellent books available at most libraries.

Understanding NLP allows us to understand the processes people use to encode and transfer their experience and to guide and modify their behaviour. All the information gathering we do is done through three sensory systems: the visual, the auditory, and kinaesthetic (feeling and touching). And to a lesser extent, we also use our senses of smell and taste, but these are not of any significance. The really interesting thing here is that visual accounts for 40% of the way we communicate, auditory only 20% and kinaesthetic 40%. Isn't that interesting?

So, what does this mean for the salesperson? Well, one of the big lessons here is to learn to match the language system used by your prospect. That way you build rapport real quickly. But be careful not to mimic their language – rather match and mirror the way they communicate.

Successful salespeople also understand the various behavioural styles people have. They understand that people fall into one of four main behavioural groups. They can be either **outgoing** in nature, or **reserved**. Or they can be either **task-oriented** or **people-oriented**.

Great salespeople have a purpose. Ever noticed that? It's true. Focus on your prospect and you'll always come out in front.

Do you have a purpose? Or have you never really thought about it? Have you always assumed you have a purpose – something like needing to sell your business so you can realise a profit and take on another business to start the whole process over again?

Sit down now and write down your own Purpose Statement. That's right – get it down on paper. Be careful not to confuse your goals with your purpose. Your goals are the more immediate things you are aiming for, like finding three likely prospects for your business, finding one that meets your franchisor's criteria, or being able to make a 25% return on your investment. Your purpose is more long-term. It touches on the very fundamentals of your existence, on what you want out of life in the broad sense. A purpose could be, for instance, to help people feel good about themselves. You see, such a purpose would involve the notion of caring for others – for your buyers. It shifts the attention away from what YOU want to what your BUYERS want.

Once you have a purpose, start selling on purpose. That's right. Sell on purpose and not by accident, and sell according to the principles of your purpose. Selling according to a fundamental purpose, like the one I've just mentioned, means you'll need to revisit your selling technique. Develop a process that ensures you sell according to the basic fundamentals of your purpose. Here's what I mean:

- Get your prospect's permission before you begin the selling process.

- Begin your selling process by asking a range of questions.

- Offer solutions to your prospect's problems.

- Seek your prospect's agreement before pushing for a decision.

- Explain the investment they are making by purchasing.

- Include a strong call to *Action*.

- Ask their permission to finalise the sale.

You see, what you're going to be doing is running through a questioning process. That's because a problem-solver's best weapon is the humble question. Not only does this help you to find out exactly what your customers want, it's a great way to build rapport. It's also a sure-fire way of having your prospect do the selling for you. You see, by working your way through a structured, and logical, sequence of questions, you'll find your prospect overcomes all the hurdles standing in the way of their decision to buy.

We all, as buyers, go through the same process whereby we investigate various options, eliminating the unsuitable as we go. What we are actually looking for during our encounters with salespeople, are reasons why we SHOULDN'T buy there and then. That's part of the 'shopping around' process. Your job, as a salesperson, is to help the buyer realise (or decide) your business is the one for them.

Remember; ask lots of open-ended questions. They're the ones that start with WHO, WHAT, WHERE, WHEN, WHY or HOW. Also be specific. Focus on the solution to their problem, and test their 'temperature' frequently to see if they are getting warmer or colder. Provide detailed answers. One of my Golden Rules to the art of asking great questions is to play dumb and dig deep. Even if you know a lot about your subject, pretend you don't. Ask the obvious and show an interest in your prospect – it will assist them in opening up on an emotional level. And remember, it's on this level that most purchasing decisions will be made.

Use question softeners. These include:

- "Can I just ask ...?"

- "By the way ...?"

- "Incidentally ...?"

There's another important reason you need to ask lots of question. It's a great, non-threatening way to keep the ball rolling. The key is to ask LOTS of questions.

Develop the habit of listening attentively to what your prospective buyers have to say. It'll make them feel like you have a genuine interest in them. Give out positive strokes. Don't just stand there looking bored, like so many salespeople do. Be enthusiastic, even if they have already intimated that they are going to buy your business. Make sure you understand the question cycle. Question – listen – positive stroke. Make this part of your routine. Get good at it and you'll be amazed at the results you'll achieve.

While asking questions, give out little pieces of information, and talk in the prospective buyer's language.

Depending on the situation or the type of business you're selling, there could be a few more important questions you need to ask. The first has to do with understanding your prospect's authority to arrive at a buying decision. Be sure to ask, "Who other than yourself will be involved in making this decision?" This is particularly relevant when selling a business with a high price tag. Then there's the matter of finances. Ask this question: "Obviously finances are very important. Can I ask what budget you've set aside for this purchase?" The answer to this will indicate whether the prospect is actually ready to make the buying decision. They may still have to visit the bank to arrange a loan, for instance.

So let's assume now you're at the stage where you can close the sale. You've reached emotion and gathered all the information you need. Ask a question that goes something like this: "Based on what you've told me (prospect's name), it appears this business may well be the solution to your long-term requirements."

When you've suggested it as a possible solution, it's time to check the prospect's temperature with a detailed question. "How does that fit with what you had in mind?"

At this stage, ASSUME THE SALE. Continue with a question something like this: "Would it be OK if I outlined what we need to get the transfer of ownership underway?" Then be silent. Silence here is your greatest asset.

Handling objections is another vital skill you'll need to master if you're going to reap the maximum benefit from buying and selling businesses.

It's particularly relevant when selling businesses. You see, selling isn't always plain sailing. Because most prospects will be looking for points of elimination (especially if they're in the early stages of their purchasing process), they'll be raising objections to your arguments. So, how do you handle these?

You do so with more questions. Get specific, with questions like these:

- "Is there any other reason besides …?"

- "If (reason) was fixed, would it be OK to go ahead?"

- If the answer is NO, there must be another reason. "Can I ask what it is?"

- If YES, "Let's invest some time looking at (reason)."

When it comes to selling, there's another rule you should bear in mind, and that is this: **Persistence Pays**. Never forget it. You see, buyers are by nature indecisive. They will be scared of making big decisions and will always want more time to think it over.

There will be instances where, despite your best efforts, the prospect just isn't willing or able to make a decision there and then. In cases like this, most salespeople write them off to experience. But don't give up. Persistence here is the key.

Keep in touch with your prospect. Show them you care. Help them work through the questions that are proving to be sticking points for them. It could be that they still have to reach a decision on whether to buy at all. It may not be your business, or even the price, that is the issue. They may have difficulties with finance or authority that needs to be resolved first. Keep close to them and assist wherever possible. Build familiarity, and rapport. That way, if they eventually do decide to go ahead, you'll be the first person they approach and not the owner of the other business they were also weighing up.

Make a point of staying in contact over the phone and through the mail. Post or fax them a brochure or any other pamphlet that you think may be relevant. And be persistent. It usually pays off in the end.

Another key characteristic of successful salespeople is that they are **professional**.

Professionalism is the hallmark of a great salesperson. The more professional you appear, the more your prospect will listen to what you have to say. People like dealing with experts in their field; with someone who knows what they're talking about. They want good advice before buying. They are afraid of being caught by some clever person whose only interest is to make money.

Being professional isn't difficult. All it takes is a genuine desire to help others to reach a buying decision, and paying some attention to detail in the following areas:

- Developing a good sales kit.

- Dressing well.

- Always being on time.

- Keeping in touch with your prospects.

- Pre-framing your prospect carefully.

- Doing your homework.

- Keeping testimonials.

- Building rapport.

- Finding out what's most important to your prospect.

- Always following-up.

- Asking for referrals.

- Sending Thank You cards.

- Being consistent.

Observe these 'rules' and you'll outshine the vast majority of salespeople out there. You'll be one step ahead of them when your prospect comes to making the decision about which business to buy.

You should now have a slightly different perspective about what real SELLING is all about. And it's no different when selling your business. You need to realise that just because it's a business you're selling and not a bar of soap, the rules of good salesmanship still apply. In fact, it's even more important you observe them because businesses aren't something people buy every day. Making a mistake is far more serious because the effects will live with them for a very long time. If you come across as being thoroughly trustworthy and likeable, then your prospective buyer will be all the more likely to believe what you say about how good the business is, what the potential is and how much opportunity you know there is for growth. It's these intangible factors that can't usually be gleaned from going through the books that very often hold the key to good business buying. Only a good salesperson can sell them to a prospective buyer.

What Else Do You Need To Be Aware Of?

Recent changes to the Franchising Code of Conduct in Australia have abolished the requirement for franchisees selling their franchise to provide a Disclosure Document to the person buying it. But if a master franchisee wishes to grant a sub-franchise to a prospective sub-franchisee, then both the franchisor and the master franchisee must provide disclosure either separately or jointly. But there appears to be grey areas here, so if this applies to you, seek legal advice first.

Brad's Top Tips For Selling A Franchise

- Make sure you actively look for a buyer even though your franchisor might have in place a program to help you exit the system. And check to see exactly what you can do yourself.

- Make sure you have all your accounting up-to-date. You see, prospective buyers will want to see what the financial state of your business is. This is what they will be most interested in.

- Be positive and continue to run the business to the best of your ability. Don't, take your eye off the ball just because you have set your heart on selling – it could take you 12 months to find the right buyer, and what will happen during these months if you slacken off? What will happen to your income stream?

- Understand your franchisor's requirements for a replacement franchisee and be very clear on what costs may be involved in selling your franchise.

- Be very clear as to why you want to sell. Ask yourself what you'll be doing next. You see, it may very well be that you are tired and need a rest, but then shouldn't you be taking a holiday? I have had a few franchisees sell up, only to return 12 months later and repurchase a franchise because they hadn't properly thought through the process. After they had sold, they took a long holiday, and then started looking for another franchise. When they realised that they couldn't find anything to compare, they realised they had made a mistake and returned. If they'd just taken some time off, they would have saved a bundle and not had to start all over again.

- You need to understand that prospective buyers will have all the same anxieties as you did when you were in the buying phase. Help them work through it.

> "Selling a business is no different to selling any other product or service – the same rules apply. It's just that they usually have a greater number of zeros in the price."
>
> **Brad Sugars**

▋ Franchising Your Business

Did you know? ... _____

Bakers Delight is the largest bakery franchise in Australasia.

It started as a single bakery in Melbourne back in 1980.

They opened their 600th bakery in November 2002.

_____

The franchise market is a dynamic industry that allows any type of business to grow by distributing products or services. When you expand by selling your trademark and business systems to another person, you adopt the franchise structure. By granting permission as a manufacturer to a distributor or retailer to sell your products, you create the contract of a franchise.

There are many reasons for you wanting to consider franchising as an option for your business. It may be that you simply want to raise a large amount of money quickly to fund future growth or a large research and development project, or you may want to ensure you have more than enough money to retire on one day. Of course, it could be that you really enjoy the challenge of building large and profitable enterprises. It could be that you get a buzz out of leading a large and diverse organisation that just happens to be of your own making. Power can be a very powerful driving force. It places you in control of a unique business entity.

Franchising is an exciting option that allows you to sell your business, over and over again without losing control of the business.

I mentioned earlier that the only real way to RICHES is through buying, building and selling businesses. Now most that follow this path to financial freedom do so by buying, building and selling one business at a time. They do one, bank the proceeds then look for the next, which they then buy, build, and sell. And so they go on.

The ULTIMATE SALE has to be to franchise the business. You see, when you have developed a sound business that works, it can be duplicated at little or no extra cost. You can sell the business time and time again to different people all over the world. And the beauty of it is there's no limit to the number of times you can sell it.

Think of some of the most popular businesses today, and chances are they're either franchises or they're business that operate under license. Take McDonalds, for instance. McDonalds is a fast food franchise that operates all over the world today. The potential is enormous, as there could just about be one in every suburb in the world. Each franchisee has a unique territory in which to operate. This ensures the franchisees do not compete with each other.

How To Go About Franchising Your Business

If you run a profitable business and are contemplating franchising, the first thing you need to decide is whether your product range or service is flexible enough to adapt to future trends. The next thing you need to decide is whether you want to franchise your business yourself, or whether you want to call in an expert business to do it for you. I'd recommend the latter for a host of reasons, not least of which is it's a complex field full of pitfalls and legalities that may not be immediately apparent.

But before you decide on whether to franchise or not, you need to consider whether this route suits you. Ask yourself the following questions:

- Do you see yourself as always striving for excellence?

- Do you possess a leadership style that can supervise and motivate a large number of people?

- Would you enjoy acting as a mentor to a large number of people?

- Are you happy to participate in forums and group activities, which could involve travel away from home?

- Are you happy to invest the money and time to continually learn new knowledge and skills to ensure your franchise system's growth?

- Are you happy to forgo your own way of doing things and follow someone else's systems?

- Are you hungry to grow your business?

- Do you have what it takes?

If you decide franchising is for you, you will need to ensure your franchise and all documentation and recommendations comply with the Franchising Code of Conduct. Effective disclosure documentation is often the catalyst for a successful franchise. You will need to ensure you have detailed disclosure documentation to ensure your franchise model is compliant with the Franchise Consumer Code and provides the potential franchisee a "no secrets" approach to buying the business.

Franchise Vs License

So what's the difference then between operating your business as a franchise or licensing it?

Basically, when you sell a franchise, you sell not only a branded business, but also the entire system with which your franchisees can run their businesses in the intended manner. You give them all the training necessary, not only to get them up and running, but also to keep them up-to-date on an on-going basis. They get all the documentation, all the reporting mechanisms and all the backing necessary to keep their performance levels in line with that which you as the franchise owner demands.

Licensing your business, on the other hand, only gives your licensees the rights to manufacture and/or market a particular product or line of products. How they set up and run your business is up to them. Major pharmaceutical products and cosmetics manufacturers often opt for this method. You see, a license is nothing more than a legal document that gives licensees official permission to do something. They are free to deliberately deviate from normally acceptable rules or practices in carrying out their business.

Both options include regular paperwork that needs to be filled in and lodged. And of course, if you are operating as a franchise or a licensed business, you will receive royalties as the owner on a regular basis.

This is what is so attractive about selling your business this way. You get to receive royalties on a regular basis. This is your CASH COW.

So, what's keeping you? Get your business started and sell ...

But there's another very good reason to take your business down the franchise route, and that's a concept called **leverage**. Let me explain ...

If you think you can earn more by working a little harder, it's time for a reality check. Take a look around you. Thousands of people you know all work hard, but are they all really getting anywhere? No, of course they're not.

The aim of the game isn't to work harder; it's to create better results with less effort. It's about finding ways of achieving more with less.

You might say the key to success is LAZINESS.

This may sound controversial, so let me explain. You need to continually leverage your time, your efforts, your money and your knowledge.

If you're paid an hourly wage, you'll never earn more than the number of hours you work, but if your business is set up so you're paid whether you work or not, you'll truly understand one of the key principles of success – leverage.

Leverage is simply the ability to do more with less.

Put it this way; employees earn money, business owners make money and investors and entrepreneurs collect money.

It's all about creating an income stream that flows whether you work or not. And creating one that gets better all the time. Franchising has got to be the ultimate business leverage tool. You see, you can sell your business over and over again, each time collecting fees, royalties and monthly payments. You do the hard work once when you set up your business ready for franchising, then the rest just happens. Each time you sell a franchise, you don't have to redo all this set-up work; it's already been done. All the systems are in place so the new business owner, the franchisee, just has to follow the system to be in business.

But at this point, let me give you a real life example of a business that has gone the franchise route.

From Small Pharmacy To International Franchise

Health Information Pharmacy is a retail pharmacy located right next door to a medical centre on Old Northern Road, Castle Hill, Sydney. It is situated away from a shopping centre, and it's a stand-alone business with hardly any traffic flow. Many of its customers are middle to high-income earners, families, some baby boomers and the elderly.

When Ken and Julia Lee took over the pharmacy in October 1998, it looked tired and was run as a traditional pharmacy – there was very little delegation and the Pharmacist did everything. The business needed a good injection of business skills. It also needed merchandising to be introduced.

At university, Ken says he was trained to be a pharmacist, not a business owner. Then once he'd qualified and begun working, he soon realised he needed to accelerate his business knowledge through coaching and mentoring. He also wanted to network with other businesses as a means of helping to improve his own business skills.

After owning the pharmacy for two years, the Lee's moment of truth arrived with the possible deregulation of the pharmaceutical industry and the introduction of discounting. It became apparent that discounting had to be done in volume for the business to survive. But Ken and Julia decided against discounting, opting instead for a policy of adding value. This meant they needed help.

Ken had just read my book *Instant Cashflow* and responded to an advertisement that *Action* Coach, Greg Albert had placed in the local newspaper.

When Ken and Julia first approached Greg, their initial goal was to try and free-up their time. They were working a 120 hour week between them. They wanted to leverage Julia out of the business first, and then Ken.

One of the challenges they faced was that the business was making a profit while they were working it, but it wouldn't if they stepped out. Obviously they wanted to change this, but they also wanted to create a business model that could be replicated through franchising.

Since teaming up with Greg and **Action**, the business has undergone a complete transformation. They created a business model that proactively takes responsibility for people's health, they developed values that are set in concrete, and they created a unique business around those values.

The core values of Health Information Pharmacy include the following:

- Reducing medication problems.

- Empowerment of people.

- Strengthening their community.

- Helping the less fortunate.

They started by doing an Alignment Consultation and setting goals (which have since changed, but were nevertheless a good start). They then embarked on a program of team training that improved their customer service levels exponentially, and developed a team incentive program called Teamaximiser™.

Teamaximiser™ is designed to give incentives to all team members based on their job description. Based on **Action's** *'5 Ways Leverage Chart'*, it also encourages companion selling and the giving out of information, while allowing the owner to know what team members are doing every hour of the day. Team members are 'penalised' for not following sales scripts or coming to work late.

One of the keys to the success of Teamaximiser™ is that there are bonuses based on individual and team performances; therefore, team members are not just working for themselves but also for a common goal.

This is powerful and works well, even without the owners being there. It has also proved highly successful at different sites.

The creation of a Unique Selling Proposition (USP) was also another system that came about through their work with *Action*. Chemconsult™ is now trademarked and is a unique pharmaceutical consulting process. The pharmacy USP fits in with the vision of the pharmacy, which is: *'Advice for a happier, longer and healthier life.'*

Through this system, Health Information Pharmacy is helping to improve patients' lives and keep people out of hospital. In 2001, there were 140,000 hospital admissions due to medication problems. And Ken and Julia believe these problems, to some extent, could have been picked up at the pharmacy level.

Through monitoring at Health Information Pharmacy, it has been shown that one in six prescriptions contain potential medication errors. Chemconsult™ picked up on them and in a large number of cases actually kept people out of hospital. This does not only benefit the patient, but it's also a major benefit to society as a whole.

The Lee's have been able to take responsibility for their business and attack it head-on. This, they say, is one amazing result of Business Coaching.

The creation of a loyalty club is another system that was developed with the help of *Action*. The Platinum Care Club is the loyalty club exclusive to Health Information Pharmacy, and it offers members more than the normal loyalty club does. Members have access to a 24-hour, seven-day a week pharmacist hotline and a local area discount book, plus they have free access to a naturopath and a $10 gift voucher for every $150 spend. It is based on a referral system, which has been fantastic for building up the customer base. This fits in well with their core values, which are:

1. Reducing medication problems. This is done through Chemconsult™.

2. Empowerment of people. This is done through the incentive program and management development program in which people are empowered to step-up to the next level.

3. Strengthening their community. Unique marketing through Strategic Area Alliances and databases make this possible.

4. Helping the less fortunate. They donate $10 to the customer's favourite charity for every three people they refer to the loyalty club. Most business owners believe they should be donating to charity, but don't have a vehicle through which to do so. This is a win-win situation that helps them grow their business while helping needy charities and people at the same time.

Health Information Pharmacy started testing and measuring everything they did. From this they stopped running newspaper ads that didn't work. They tested and measured headlines as well as guarantees. And while some of the guarantees got them into trouble with the Pharmacy Board, because the Pharmacy Act didn't allow them, Ken viewed this as a valuable lesson, as it put them right on track! It also helped them ascertain how far they could go in marketing, yet stay with their core values, as well as the industry guidelines.

Pharmacists were also employed as managers. Systems and Key Performance Indicators were set up to track performances and Ken's routine changed dramatically. He went from working IN the business to working ON it, and now he is working on other people's businesses through franchising. He has also had the ability to create and be creative within the pharmacy setting.

After three months, Julia had started to leverage herself out of the business. After six months she was totally out. After 12 months Ken was also totally out, although it took another 12 months to franchise the business.

The business outlook is great – the business sees itself as being very community-based and as a hub for community activities, especially in the health care arena. There is a naturopath in store. They also have strategic alliances with a chiropractor, massage therapist, gym, restaurant, real estate agent, financial planner and even holiday destinations.

The business culture is excellent. There is a strong culture within the business and externally as well. The pharmacy has been accepted quite well in the community, especially considering it was one of the first pharmacies to be accredited under quality care in Australia, with various press releases and articles being written about the work they are doing. In fact, through the work he has done with **Action**, Ken was nominated for *Young Australian of the Year 2000*.

"The pharmacy was making profit before we took over, but we have doubled the net profit in the last three years," says Ken. Turnover increased by 52% (from a large base), profit by 42% and average dollar sale from $30 to $46.

"And although there were not many targets in the early days, Health Information Pharmacy has now been vigorously setting them for the next 12 months. Ideally, the target is domination in the marketplace. We have a strong financial position and a good aggressive group in terms of marketing and pharmaceutical care and how we position ourselves in the market."

However, not everything has been a smooth run. There have been several challenges, which include a car going through the front window of the store one week before accreditation and a landlord who tried to close down the store. Then there were some challenges with the Pharmacy Board regarding some of their marketing strategies.

But the main challenge was discount pharmacies opening in the local area, and in some respects, this is what led Ken and Julia to choose the direction they did. Of course, like every other business, there were also staffing challenges that involved key team members leaving. The positive here is that other team members stepped up and accepted the challenge.

The end result has been massive. There is now a fully systemised business with over 100 systems. A 6-volume manual has been created that covers all areas of the business from finance to HR, and from dispensing to management and ownership. This has become a turnkey business for many pharmacists. The owners no longer work in-store, but still know what is happening.

A successful business model based on marketing, merchandising and team incentives has been developed. Health Information Pharmacy has shown that their systems and models can work in Castle Hill, and they are duplicating them throughout their franchise network.

Ken has taken an office in nearby Norwest Business Park, in Baulkham Hills, NSW and works purely on developing the franchise. However, he says this is just the beginning for Health Information Pharmacy, as they are now taking the business to the next level – from state to nationwide before going international.

Taking it to the next level is going to be traumatic, as Ken says he will be stepping out of the comfort zone of being a pharmacist once again to leading pharmacists, some of whom have a lot more experience in the industry than he does. "But I am looking forward to the challenge of making a difference in multiple areas," he says. "We will be sharing our values and beliefs throughout the pharmaceutical industry, and it's going to help patients."

And what of the future?

"It has been an exciting time with Greg Albert, my Business Coach. I'm looking forward to big things in the future. Greg is still involved as my coach, some two and a half years on, and he is also now the Business Development Manager at Health Information Pharmacy. One thing we have insisted on is that as each franchisee comes on board, they get a Business Coach for at least three months to ensure their success. I would recommend this as a must for any franchise out there. Working with *Action* has been incredible for the business. Every business owner should take it up because it is an investment in his or her own knowledge and skill development."

The Structure You've Got To Use

If you're going to franchise your business, then there's one structure you've simply got to use. You see, if you can't make at least a few million from this, you'll have to kick yourself, it's that easy.

The structure I'm now going to tell you about works extremely well and it's simple. That's the beauty of it. I became a trendsetter using this system. This is how it works:

You franchise your business, not to a myriad of franchisees but to a handful of master franchisees, who in turn franchise their business to franchisees in their territory. In my case, I first sold master franchises for the various Australian states to master licensees, who in turn sold franchises to franchisees in their states. These franchisees, who became primary franchisees, are able to, in turn, sell associate franchises. This enables them to develop a passive income stream from their businesses.

In effect you are setting up a structure that is multi-layered.

In Australia, master franchises were sold along state lines, but in overseas markets, I sold master franchises for each country I expanded into. This way, I don't really get too involved in the nitty gritty of running the business in these areas; my master licensees (as they are known) are responsible for the smooth running of the business in their territories. It is up to them to do everything from selling franchises to supporting the franchisees. Head Office provides training and ongoing strategic assistance, direction and global communication.

Brad's Top Tips For Franchising A Business

- Make sure your concept has been thoroughly tested to make certain all the systems work and that the business is running smoothly and profitably. Will it stand the test of time or become another business statistic? This is best done by running a pilot successfully first.

- Make certain the business lends itself to being duplicated and that a demand exists for your product or service. Make certain too that your brand is recognised in the marketplace.

- Consult your lawyer, financial advisor (both of whom must have franchise experience) and a franchise consultant. Make sure you have all your legals in place before you franchise the business.

- Produce a set of comprehensive operational manuals, and test to see that they are understandable and that they work. Make sure your manuals take a step-by-step approach and don't assume your franchisees know anything. Put absolutely everything down in the manuals.

- Have an experienced franchise solicitor draw up your franchise agreements.

- Make sure you have enough cash in your budget to sustain the business at least through the first three years, or until you begin to see profits flowing through the system.

- Design your training and support systems system very well. Seek professional help if necessary. Have them in place before you begin franchising – you can't build these as you go because then your first few franchisees will think they are the guinea pigs. Understand that it is the systems that they are actually buying, so if you don't have tried and tested systems in place, what are you selling?

- Think carefully about how you are going to select who you sell your franchises to. How are you going to determine who is suitable and who is not? This is most important as the results and experiences of your first few franchisees will determine the longer-term success of your business. If they fail, chances are so will your business, but if they are a roaring success, your business will flourish. So think carefully about this: are you chasing money so you can expand your business rapidly, or are you looking for certain qualities in your franchisees? If so, what are they? Remember, these people will set the ball rolling for you.

- Design marketing and PR systems that are above reproach. They must be as professional as possible.

- Give alot of thought to how you are going to cultivate your relationships with your franchisees so it can remain as cordial as it possibly can. Much is going to depend on this and if your system is lacking here, it is going to severely test you in the years to come. Keep your lines of communication as open as possible.

- How are you going to ensure your franchisees are able to remain at the forefront on their market? What provisions have you to ensure your research and development is as good as it can be? And will this be good enough?

- Do you understand The Franchising Code Of Conduct? It is mandatory in Australia.

- Make sure you have a detailed and up-to-date folder on every franchisee in your system. Keep everything documented. You see, franchising involves relationships, and these relationships are both personal and legal. And they come unstuck every now and then. So document everything, not to trap anyone, but rather to cover yourself should you end up in court. Include sign-offs in your system so franchisees can sign that they are happy with things as they work their way through the system. For instance, on completion of initial training, get them to sign a form stating they are satisfied with the quality of training received. Be in a good position to put forward your case, if required to.

- Learn as much as you can about the anxieties franchisees face before they purchase a franchise, when they make the purchase and as they work as a franchisee.

- Make certain your system is adaptable and able to take on board suggestions and experiences from your franchisee base. Remember, a franchise system is just like a tree; it's either growing or it's dying. It simply can't stay the way it is *ad infinitum*.

The bottom line here is you need to be well prepared before taking your business down the franchise path. If you're not, you could end it fighting lengthy and costly legal battles. Nobody wants these and besides, if your business fails, it will be precisely the opposite result of what you were hoping to achieve in the first place.

Failure is not part of the plan. If this is where your franchise hopes end, you'll have to seriously question whether you planned to fail, or failed to plan.

Common Mistakes

It is a good thing to at least THINK about failure before you get underway with the franchising of your business. You see, if you knew the main reasons why many franchise operations fail, do you think that could help you not to make the same mistakes? Do you think you could plan early so you have systems in place to ensure the chances of you making the same mistakes are minimised? You bet.

So what are the most common mistakes franchisors make?

Probably the most well publicised is greed. What many of them seem to want is quick cash. The greed factor has led to many spectacular crashes in recent times that have left a trail of bitter, disappointed and broke franchisees who have lost everything. These highly publicised disasters have given franchising a bad name, but fortunately things are getting better; the authorities have introduced legislation to regulate the industry and the industry itself has developed a far more responsible attitude towards business in recent times.

The next reason some franchisors fail is due to poor selection techniques when selling franchises. This is probably related to the greed factor because all some franchisors are interested in is selling franchises. They are only interested in their own cashflow situation. Selling franchises is fine, but for the long-term sustainability of the system, it pays to be very selective when choosing who to sell franchises to. You see, get this wrong and you'll end up with disgruntled franchisees beginning to quit simply because it wasn't for them. It wasn't their cup of tea. And disgruntled franchisees start talking to others and saying things tinged with emotion and bad feeling. It does your business no good at all because word can spread like wild fire. Other franchisees who might be 'sitting on the fence' or going through a rough patch might get caught up in this and talk themselves into failure. You need to bear in mind that, in franchising, the situation can develop rightly or wrongly into "it's you against them" – the franchisor against the franchisees. This is just a fact of the business, because the two entities really do have different aims and ambitions, even though their overall goal would be the same. You can think of it much the same as the classic boss-worker analogy.

Franchises fail due to insufficient or poor training. They aren't sufficiently equipped to tackle what lies in store for them. They return from initial training knowing no better, but pumped up with enthusiasm. They are ready to make their mark on the business world, but when situations arise that they are ill-prepared to take on, they begin to feel incompetent and inferior. Only this time they have no one to turn to, because they will by now be having doubts about you, the franchisor. You see, if you let them down by not training them properly, what else will you be neglecting to do? Will you be able to satisfactorily assist them with day-to-day operational matters? You will have lost their trust and confidence, and from here on in, it's usually just a matter of time before you loose them altogether.

The stagnation of new product research and development is also a major reason some franchise systems fail. It might be all well and good when the business is initially franchised, but as time goes by, the business environment will change and your business must keep pace with changing times. You must equip your franchisees with the tools necessary to compete in the marketplace. You must help them to stay competitive and in business.

Some franchises make such rapid inroads when they first appear on the scene that the owners begin to believe their system is so good they can expand at a meteoric pace indefinitely. The simple truth is few can. Growing too quickly can be the downfall of even the best franchise system in the world. It's like any business that's growing too quickly – the first problem they'll experience is a cashflow shortage. That's right, even though they have customers pouring in through the doors, they will find their cash beginning to dry up, because they'll be purchasing stock and investing in enlarging their facilities so they can handle the extra demand, all of which costs money, yet profit takes time to work its way down through the system and into their coffers. I know this may seem like a contradiction in terms, but it's true. Growing too quickly can be really disastrous.

Franchisors that fail to continuously test and measure the performance of their franchisees often only realise there is a problem when it's too late. The secret is to have systems in place that measure their performances on a regular, on-going basis. That way all that is needed is a small tweaking here and there to keep them on track. It's often more efficient and less painful to make a series of small corrections than one large one. It's also less costly.

The final reason some franchise systems fail is that they don't pay nearly enough attention to developing meaningful relationships with their franchisees. This results in a breakdown of communications in the true sense of the word; there isn't nearly as much openness and trust in the business between the various players, leading to conflict. Conflict, when not handled properly or resolved only ends up in litigation, which no one really wants.

The Secret Of One Franchisor's Success

Let's look now at what the secret has been for one of the world's top franchises – Subway. "The appeal of a Subway franchise is universal – with low investment, a simple operation, and unparalleled support for the franchisees," says Don Fertman, Subway's Director of Franchise Sales. And according to the franchise's President and co-founder Fred DeLuca, "We have a very simple approach to business. What's really great about our team is that they keep analysing the market, they do a lot of research and testing and stay focused for the benefit of all our franchise owners."

To succeed as a franchisor, it's imperative that you remain responsive to new ideas."

Brad Sugars

▌Franchising – A Question Of Relationships

Did you know? ... _____

Bob Jane T-Marts was a pioneer of the Australian franchise industry.

First established in 1965, Bob Jane T-Marts now has over 140 outlets.

The first Bob Jane T-Marts franchise outlet opened in Artarmon, NSW in 1972 and is still trading successfully today.

The business really had its roots in motor racing, when Bob Jane began importing special racing tyres for his racing cars back in 1962.

_____

Franchising is really all about relationships. This is what it all boils down to. Make sure you develop great, lasting relationships and you will be giving yourself every chance of making a success of your franchise business.

But let's go into this a little deeper.

The first thing you need to think about is what your motive was for buying a franchise? Or if you haven't bought it yet, why are you thinking of buying one in the first place?

Understand this, and you'll be on the right path when it comes to deciding how you can approach this issue of relationships. Get this clear in your mind and you'll have a clearer picture of the role relationships play in the world of franchising.

Why would you want to go into business for yourself? Just look at the statistics. Around 80% of businesses started this year will be gone in five years time.

Most business owners seem to work harder than any of their people and many seem to earn less than they could make elsewhere.

From what I've found, people start their own business for one thing and one thing only: FREEDOM. Whether that be working for themselves, having more time to themselves, financial freedom, or just the freedom of knowing that they're in charge of their life.

They have a longing to be in charge. They want to 'do it their way'. They want to be responsible for their own destiny. Now all this is absolutely fine; it's fantastic and it's positive, but it's not going to just happen for you because you have made this great big important decision. Your life won't miraculously change the way you want it to.

Travelling down the road of life, it's easy to be distracted, to get off track and lose sight of the big picture. What's the old saying? "Can't see the forest for the trees." However, every day you're getting little taps on the shoulder, an idea that you should change what you're doing, a suggestion from someone, a hint, and you either learn to take the taps, or eventually they become signposts you run into.

And the signposts are a whole lot bigger and they hurt a whole lot more. Then if you're still too blind, too stubborn or just too stupid to read the signs, you'll stray into the path of oncoming traffic and get run over by the proverbial Mack truck.

Why do you think that most successful people are great networkers? Why do they seem to have great relationships with friends and colleagues? It's because they've perfected the craft of surrounding themselves with other people and then listening – *really* listening – to what they have to say. They have developed these relationships to the point that they have EARNED the right to ask others for advice. They can in one night absorb more 'taps on the shoulder' than many take on board in a whole year. Just remember to get the facts, listen for the taps and look for the signs. Sticking your head in the sand never helped anyone.

When you think about it, you can't survive in business without paying particular attention to the relationships you have with others. It's like the lifeblood of business. You need to understand that, whether you like it or not, you WILL have relationships with a whole range of people. You see, if you dislike the idea and believe you are the shy type who prefers to get on with things alone, then the relationships you have with others will be cold and aloof. You will come across as unfriendly and uncooperative. Relationships are something you can't avoid – they develop whether you like it or not. And here's another thing to consider: relationships can be worked on so that they take the shape and form you want them to take. And it takes just as much effort to develop good relationships with others as it does to develop bad ones. It costs nothing to smile at someone, to be friendly and polite. The choice is yours. It all depends really on how successful you want to be in business.

When it comes to examining the types of relationships a business has, it is convenient to categorise them into two distinct groups; external relationships and internal relationships. Let's look at them separately.

External Relationships

The very basic form of relationship any business develops is with those who deal with it. And the first manifestation of it is through another well known, but often poorly implemented concept; customer service. You see, it's through the service you give to your customers that they begin to form their first impressions of you or your business. And it's these impressions that drive your relationship with them.

So let's look a little closer at the concept of customer service. Let's take it one word at a time.

Who Is 'The Customer'?

So who then is your customer?

If you really begin to think about it, there are four classes, or types, of customer and they're all equally important to you. Who are they? They include:

- The Owners: Business must serve them by providing an acceptable level of profit.

- The Team: Business must serve them by providing recognition, rewards and a pay cheque.

- The Suppliers: Business must serve them by paying their bills.

- The Customers: Business must serve them by filling their needs.

As you can see, customers are a diverse group of people that come from all walks of life. They also have various, and differing, relationships with the business. They do have one thing in common, however. They all have needs and wants.

The needs and wants of the owners will be different to those of the team, and suppliers will certainly have different needs and wants to those who buy from the business. But they all have needs and wants. It's the job of the business to discover what those are, and then to sell them what they need.

Of course, they will be selling rather differently to Owners of the business then they would to Suppliers. Selling takes place on different levels. The Team have to be 'sold' on the business; otherwise they'd leave and look for better employment, if they didn't believe the business had a future. Owners could sell their shares if they weren't 'sold' on the businesses outlook by the Management Team. And Suppliers wouldn't offer generous credit terms or prices if the business wasn't 'sold' to them correctly at the outset.

You need to understand the concept of providing great Customer Service is all about relationship building – and this means communication.

It's a two-way street that involves an Emotional Bank Account in which you make deposits and withdrawals. You need to establish your Emotional Bank Account with your customers by first making a deposit, much as you would an ordinary bank account. You would, for instance, make a deposit of trust, goodwill, price incentives or the offer of a good job. Then, after you have built up a positive account through showing your customers you are genuinely interested in their needs and wants, you can begin making withdrawals. You can, only then, begin expecting your customers to begin assisting you to achieve your own goals, helping you reach your sales targets, referring friends or becoming Raving Fans.

Who Is Your Ideal Customer?

It's often said there are customers, and there are customers. How true this is.

There are those customers you'd love to deal with every day, and there are those you'd wish never came back. But there are more than just two basic groups. There are, in fact, four categories; A, B, C and D. I explain them as follows:

- **A**wesome

- **B**asic

- **C**an't deal with

- **D**ead

You might wish to only deal with the A's and B's. If that's the case, get rid of the rest. How do you do that? Simple. Tell them. Or set up rules for doing business, then write to everyone on your database, explaining you're repositioning your business and here are the new rules. You can also change your pricing policy or the décor of your premises – this alone will filter out those you don't want. A video store wanted to shake off the young hooligans who had taken to gathering there. All they did was to change the type of music they played in the store. Instead of playing music teenagers listen to, they began playing classical music. Their client base changed virtually overnight.

If you were to really analyse your business, you'll find that 20% of your customers account for 80% of your business. This is what I call, the 80-20 Rule. Do you know who your 20% is? These are the one's you should be concentrating your efforts on.

Satisfaction

Now that we've looked at the first word in 'Customer Service,' let's look at what lies behind the second. Begin by asking yourself this: do customers leave your business feeling satisfied or delighted?

I know this is a profound question, but you do need to give it some thought. Be honest with yourself. How do your customers really feel about doing business with you?

The first thing you need to understand is that customers EXPECT to be satisfied when making contact with any business. They have a need they want satisfied. They've also gone to the trouble of finding out which businesses can satisfy their need, then they've done something about it – they've either phoned up or actually travelled to your business. What happens next will determine the lasting impression they have of your business.

They EXPECT satisfaction, but will actually talk to others about your business if they get more than they EXPECT.

So give them something to talk about.

This is the first step to creating a great relationship with them; one that will result in them becoming what I call a Raving Fan.

Good Customer Service is Pro-Active. Don't wait until you have a problem in this area before doing something about it – before you think about ways and means of taking care of your customers. How can you give your customers something more than they expect?

Think of different things you could do to get them talking. Brainstorm. Consult your sales people. Start becoming innovative in this area. Think outside the square.

Make this part of your routine. Get used to constantly searching for new ways of satisfying your customers. Keep your eyes open, watch what other businesses are doing, and keep innovating. You see, customers actually EXPECT you to keep getting better.

Moments Of Truth

Do you know what your Moments Of Truth are? They are the times when it really counts to impress someone with your service.

Do you now know what yours might be? Take the time now to list as many of them as you can. Be ruthless with yourself. A good place to start is with your customer interaction.

Once you've jotted down some of your Moments Of Truth, you'll begin to see why customers leave you for a competitor. You'll begin to develop ideas to stop this in its tracks.

Before we go any further, here are some statistics about why customers leave that may startle you. They are:

- 1% due to death.

- 3% due to a house move.

- 5% due to buying from a friend.

- 9% due to being sold by a competitor.

- 14% due to finding a better product or price.

- 68% due to perceived indifference.

These figures are staggering. 68% of your customers leave because they perceive your business to be indifferent to their needs. They feel you just don't care.

Now look at how many leave because of the efforts of your opposition. The figures are so small as to be almost negligible. Only 9% are swayed by the active efforts of your competitors, while a mere 14% find a more attractive deal elsewhere.

Remember my 80-20 Rule? If you were to really do well with only 20% of your customers, you'd be looking after those that account for 80% of your revenue. So how hard is it to hang on to that 68% slice of customers who leave just because they think you don't care about them? Putting this another way, how easy would it be to retain that 20% of customers who contribute the most to your bottom line just by treating them decently? Why do all the difficult (and costly) things to shore up your bottom line when a simple remedy like offering great customer service can do it for you?

Winning Customer Service

OK, so you've decided the level of service your business provides its customers could be a whole lot better. What do you do about it to make it the talk of the town?

Let me now share with you the three steps you must take to achieving great, and meaningful, customer service.

Step 1. You must aim for CONSISTENCY. It's no good if whatever you do differs each day. Your customers will want to know that whenever they visit your business the service will be the same. And it doesn't matter what the level of customer service is, so long as it's consistent. I mean if you are running a five star hotel you will serve your dinner guests at their tables, whereas if you were running a fast food outlet you wouldn't. This doesn't mean the customer service at the fast food joint is inferior to that at the hotel. It would just be different; at a different level. And you must offer consistency in both service and delivery.

Step 2. Make it EASY for customers TO BUY. You see, with consistency comes TRUST. By building consistency into your sales process, you will ensure that you systematically surpass their expectations every time they buy from you. They will begin to trust your business; they will know every time they buy from you there will be no unpleasant surprises. They receive the same pleasant greeting each and every time they arrive, they receive the same efficient and courteous service while they are there and their questions are answered accurately and honestly. Do everything possible to make their buying experience easy. This way, they will know what to expect when they return next time.

Step 3. Now introduce the WOW Factor. This is the way to create Raving Fans. Understand this: the fundamentals of creating great customer service involve creating a system to make sure your customer's expectations are surpassed, every time. Having satisfied customers implies you have given them all they've wanted, and nothing more. But if you're going to surpass their expectations, you must systematically go beyond their expectations. Every single day you need to be getting better. The Japanese have a good term for this. They call it Kaisen – constant and never ending improvement.

To do this, you need to go further than just providing great customer service. You need to implement a customer service plan, which comprises the following action points:

- Identify your ideal customers. Find out who they are.

- Create your customer service vision. Remember, customer service is about understanding that little things are important. You need to make an impression on your customers.

- Conduct market research. You need to ask your ideal customers what they would regard as excellent customer service.

- Now create your customers' customer service vision.

- Take the two visions and combine them to create an ultimate customer service vision.

- Decide what it is you can promise your customers. This must be something you can deliver each and every time. My rule is to under promise and over deliver.

- Make sure you get your team involved. Give them the vision, and ask them for ideas on how it can be delivered. Work consistently with them on this.

- Make sure you have continual check-ups. Make sure you are delivering what you promise.

- As your level of service gets better, move the goal posts. Keep improving.

- Always give your customers more than they expect. I send out free gifts continually.

- And always smile. You see, people love to feel special.

People are willing to PAY for service – when it's the service they desire. If the service exceeds their expectations, they will STAY with you and they will SAY good things about your business.

But if your service is poor, they'll WALK away, they'll TALK negatively about your business, and they'll BAULK at coming back.

Be consistent, always smile and give your customer's more than they expect. That way you can be sure they'll leave with a smile on their face.

The Ladder Of Loyalty

Most good businesses spend time and money in the pursuit of good customer service so they can get customers to come back and make further purchases. But understand good customer service in itself doesn't build customer loyalty. Take, as an example, two businesses. One gives average customer service and the other prides itself on its good customer service. If the first business writes a follow-up letter to its customers inviting them to shop there again whereas the second one doesn't, where do you think the customers are more likely to shop next? At the first business, even though its customer service is rated as only being average.

OK, so let's take a closer look at this very important concept – customer loyalty.

How do you build loyal customers? I like to explain this using the Loyalty Ladder concept. What I mean by this is you have to move your customers up this ladder, and you need to keep them moving up the ladder all the time.

Think of it just like an ordinary ladder. If you were to step up onto the first rung of the ladder, would you just hang around there for a while before doing something? No, you would want to climb up straight away, or get off.

Now, ask yourself why it is you want to build a Loyalty Ladder for your business. I'd suggest it is because the first sale you make to a customer is made at a loss. Yes, statistics show that nine out of ten first sales are made at a loss, because there are advertising costs, marketing costs and commissions that first need to be taken into account. If you don't get that customer to come back and buy again, that customer isn't profitable to you.

Let's now take a closer look at the Loyalty Ladder and what the various stages on it involve:

```
┌─────────────────────┐
│     RAVING FAN       │
├─────────────────────┤
│      Advocate        │
├─────────────────────┤
│       Member         │
├─────────────────────┤
│      Customer        │
├─────────────────────┤
│       Shopper        │
├─────────────────────┤
│      Prospect        │
├─────────────────────┤
│       Suspect        │
└─────────────────────┘
```

1. **SUSPECT.** When they first start out on the Loyalty Ladder, right at the bottom rung, people are called suspects. How do you identify them? They are only potential customers at this stage, they fit within your target market and they are willing to buy from you if they are in your geographic area.

2. **PROSPECT.** We then move up the ladder to prospect. A prospect is a suspect who has taken some sort of action like phoning from an ad or visiting your business. You must collect all their details so you can stay in touch. This is most important, as building customer loyalty is all about relationship building. You will be aiming to build a database of prospects. You now use all your sales skills to move your prospect one rung up the ladder to the next stage, to that of customer.

3. **CUSTOMER.** To be classified as a customer, your prospect needs to have spent money, and you need to have recorded the sale in

your records. This last step may seem strange, but it is most important, because it allows you to differentiate between prospects and customers on your database. You see, if you are planning to send a letter out to all prospects offering them an incentive to buy, you don't want to be sending it to people who are already customers. This record will also tell you when they last bought, how often they buy and what their average dollar sale is. Here's something you'll find interesting: I find most businesses put up a huge STOP sign at this level. The salespeople seem to sit back waiting for these customers to return, instead of taking proactive action and inviting them back. Understand that at the customer level, they have cost you money. If you are content to stop at this level, your business will eventually go broke. I have eaten out at many restaurants, and guess what? I'm not on any database. I've never received a letter from any of them saying: "Brad, we'd love to have you back." This is, to my mind, quite insane. They seem to be saying; "You've bought, now I'm going to just hope like heck you come back." Think about the possibilities for your business. The STOP sign is the scariest thing I've come across in business. You need to get rid of it, and fast.

4. **MEMBER.** When your customers make their second purchase, they become members. They now have a feeling of belonging. Understand customers who make two purchases are ten times more likely to make more than someone who has only made one. So, you need to put some effort into your members. Give them a membership card and a membership pack. How many of your customers know all your products? Very few, I would suggest. So why not include a product catalogue in the membership pack? You can also include samples, vouchers and things like that. One interesting example I came across recently was at a truck stop in New Zealand. The owner pinned up photographs on a notice board of all drivers who had stopped the night there. Then there's the coffee shop that gives you your own personalised coffee mug. Each time you come in, they get your mug down from the shelf for you. These two examples give members a sense of belonging.

5. **ADVOCATE.** Once you have members, you move them up the ladder to the next level – to that of advocate. An advocate is someone who sells you to other people. The criteria for an advocate are they will give referrals or promote you, and they keep buying. Advocates are one of your major capital assets.

6. **RAVING FAN.** Once you have created an advocate, you need to move them up to the top of the ladder where they become raving fans. Understand the difference: an advocate is someone who will sell for you whereas a raving fan is someone who can't stop selling for you. The exciting thing about Raving Fans is they can almost be regarded as part of your team. They want to see you succeed. Of course, they continue buying from you all along.

Remember, the aim of the game is to move people up from Customer to Raving Fan. This is where you begin to make profit. And remember, people are prepared to PAY for service.

We have now looked at your external relationships in some detail, but this is just one aspect of the relationships you will need to concentrate on. You also have internal relationships that are just as important. You see, the way to interact with your internal stakeholders, your staff and your franchisor, is just as important as your relationship with your external stakeholders, your customers.

Internal Relationships

Many businesspeople have the misguided impression that just because what goes on inside their business isn't visible to the public, it is not important and of no concern to anyone other than those who work there. What rubbish.

This is where many go wrong. The way you get along with the members of your team is vitally important to the well being of your business. It's just like the importance of having a healthy heart. Just because it's inside you and can't be seen doesn't mean it can be ignored. Let's look now at some of the important things you need to consider to ensure you establish internal relationships that are conducive to the development of a healthy, vibrant business.

Culture

To begin with, one of the most important strategic moves you can make when buying or establishing a new business is to think about the culture you'd like your business to adopt. Ask all your team members to contribute as this allows them to buy in and identify with the business in a fundamental way. After all, they are the ones that will be the life and soul of the business on a day-to-day basis. They need to feel comfortable working there and they need to be happy with their working environment.

Once you have reached a consensus on this, write it down and display it prominently at key locations in your work place.

Remember, your company's culture starts with you. You set the tone and the standards. This was one of the very first things I did when I established **Action** *International.* I had my team come up with what we call our 12 Points of Culture. Everyone adheres to them, and they are explained to all prospective team members when we hold our interviews. That way they know the environment they will be hoping to join and the culture they will be fitting into.

We also hold all our interview sessions as group sessions where all members of our team participate together in group interviews which take the form of a de-selection process. You see, we believe that because we pride ourselves in having FANTASTIC internal relationships, every team member has an equal say in who comes to work here. They all have to, after all, get along with new additions to our team. We also interview all aspiring team members TOGETHER in a group, so that we all can weigh up the different personality types in an effective way. We spend the first half of the interview session outlining what our company does and what our goals and mission are. We also explain in detail what our 12 Points of Culture are. Then each member of the team has a chance to outline their role within the company and what their experience has been working for the company. They also talk about how the team fits together and how they work together, both in busy times and in times when things are a little more relaxed. They talk about the good and the bad in an unthreatening atmosphere.

Then after a short break, the interviewees are asked to answer three basic questions, one person at a time. This is done in the group situation so that every interviewee can listen to what the others say. Some find it intimidating, as they aren't used to being open and others are put out, as they aren't used to talking in front of a large group of strangers. This is part of our de-selection process and we make it clear that anyone can slide out at any time should they feel they won't fit in. The end result is we always end up with fantastic people working for the company; people who share common beliefs and outlooks and who are prepared to work together to achieve common goals. Another result of this process is that all our team members feel they can, from the moment they join, work in an open environment where real, effective two-way communication is encouraged. Nobody has anything to hide and can feel free to ask for help or discuss challenges or concerns before they become major stumbling blocks.

This culture of openness is further encouraged through our weekly WIFLE sessions that take place every Friday afternoon. The idea is that everybody gets a turn to speak to the group in an uninterrupted and open forum, free from the threat of reprisals or repercussions. WIFLE stands for **W**hat **I F**eel **L**ike **E**xpressing. This is the forum for getting things off your chest or for expressing thanks for help received. What is said in session stays there and is not spoken about again afterwards. The sessions end by everyone 'Whooshing" it away for good.

Now that's a look at our culture. Of course, every company will have a different culture and that's fine. As long as it reflects the collective feelings, likes and dislikes, and ways of going about business, that's OK.

Every business will have a culture. It's just that some cultures just develop all on their own because nobody takes charge and directs the way it comes about. And chances are, these haphazard cultures don't do anything positive for the business. They usually just evolve as time goes by, incorporating many counter-productive elements like a propensity for gossip, for office politics to become a dominant factor, or for bullying to rule the roost.

The scary thing about company culture is that once established it's extremely difficult to change. Usually the only way to effect a change is by getting rid of your team (or most of them) and starting again. This, as you can imagine, is a very expensive option.

Who Are Your Internal Stakeholders?

Your internal stakeholders are people or organisations that have a direct interest in your business. They are 'insiders' by virtue of their relationship with you. They are not clients or customers, although they could be IN ADDITION to being internal stakeholders. They have a vested interest in seeing you succeed.

So, who then will you classify as internal stakeholders?

They include:

- Team members

- Shareholders

- Directors

- Contractors

- Sub contractors

- Suppliers

- Your franchisor

- Your franchisees

- Affiliates

There could be more, depending on your situation. Make a note of those that apply to your business by putting names next to the categories. Then jot down next to each the weighting you'd give as an internal stakeholder. Some, like team members and franchisees, will rate 100%, while others, like shareholders, directors and your franchisor may rate 100% depending on whether they have any other interests or relationships. Contractors and sub contractors too may rate 100%. Others may only be rated at 10% or 20%.

Going through this exercise will reveal an interesting relationships graph that you can use to tailor your communication effort. It will also help you to ensure you aren't leaving anyone out of the communication loop.

Internal Communication

Communications is the lifeblood of any company. And just as healthy blood needs to flow through clear, open veins, so too must a company have a policy of open communication channels for healthy communication to exist.

Furthermore, in order to facilitate effective communications, a good, trusting and non-threatening relationship must exist between all parties.

What exactly is effective communications then?

Effective communication exists when the sender of a message receives sufficient feedback from the recipient of that message to indicate that the contents of the message was fully received and understood. Or to put it another way; effective communication is the result you get. If you're not getting the response you want, you're not communicating correctly. Get it?

Internal communications is such an important area for business that it has become a specialist area in its own right. It is now recognised that good internal relations leads to good internal communications, which in turn results in reduced internal conflict, increased harmony and a greater understanding of the goals that need to be achieved. Get this right and you are well on your way to creating a successful business.

Internal communication occurs within a system whereas external communication occurs between external systems. I have used the word system here in preference to organisation because some internal stakeholders might actually belong to another business but be considered an internal stakeholder by virtue of their interest in the business. Internal communication also exists on various levels; the interpersonal level, the intragroup level and the intraorganisational level.

What is the purpose of internal communications? Why is it so important? Why can't we just communicate as and when we need to?

Internal communication basically has four main functions, which are:

- To manage information.

- To manage the identification of problems and solutions.

- To manage conflict.

- To manage and regulate behaviour.

As you can see, it covers a wide range of important areas. Get your internal communication wrong and you can expect problems on a wide front, but get it right and you'll join an exclusive group of companies that enjoys a fantastic working relationship with all their stakeholders. Internal harmony leads to greatly increased productivity and efficiency, which, in turn, will manifest itself on your bottom line.

Understanding Human Behaviour

The way organisations communicate is so important. It affects not only their ability to promote themselves and get potential customers to take notice and consider them when needing to buy something, it also affects their ability to actually convert these prospects into actual customers. Once that is done, the way the business communicates further with their customers will dictate whether they buy from them again or increase the amount of money they spend.

Of course, an organisation's ability to communicate also influences the morale of its team members and other stakeholders. Disgruntled team members aren't likely to 'go the extra mile' for any business and as a result, that little bit of extra profit that could have been made from a transaction will slip you by.

Most large corporations understand the need for good communication in general and even better internal communication in particular. That's why they have whole departments assigned to look after it. They have Public Relations Departments, Communication Departments, Consumer

Relations Departments, Internal Affairs Departments and Corporate Communications Departments. But what of small businesses? How many of them spend any time on this vital subject? How many claim they can't afford the luxury?

Luxury? It's a necessity. You see, they should really be saying the one thing they can't afford is to go broke.

Understand that, in order to make internal communication one of your strengths and not weaknesses, you don't need to create a whole department that will be staffed by experts. It can be handled on a very basic level, because it is really only basic human behaviour. Get in the habit of communicating openly with all your internal stakeholders and make open communication part of your company's culture. Get everyone involved. Take away their fear of 'opening themselves up' by ensuring there are no recriminations for being open and honest.

The first thing you need to do to accomplish this is to understand as much as you can about human behaviour.

Human behaviour can be approached from two basic viewpoints; the psychological and the social. These two approaches are not new; they go back to the ancient Greeks. Aristotle emphasised the individual and Plato favoured understanding human behaviour by studying their social relations. Then, in the 19th century, a new approach came into fashion when the philosopher August Compte proposed a mix of the two approaches. He favoured studying both individual and social behaviour.

All three approaches are useful when it comes to understanding how people behave in organisations. The psychological perspective looks at how individuals affect others and how they affect the organisation. The sociological perspective looks at how organisations affect the behaviour of individual people, and the integrative perspective looks at how both organisations and individuals interact with each other.

Let's take a quick look at these different approaches as a means of highlighting some of the factors you need to consider when designing your communication processes.

Psychological Approach

The type of variables that affect the way individuals communicate include the way they see themselves in their work situation, their level of reluctance to communicate, and their level of satisfaction when communicating. People continue working for an organisation just as long as it meets their individual needs.

Sociological Approach

The organisation's social structure, the relationships they have with the group, the amount of influence they enjoy and the communication networks they belong to affect their communication behaviour. This approach maintains that the way people behave is determined by the limits placed on them by the organisation, or society in general. The social environment in which they live determines their behaviour.

Integrative Approach

This approach says that people communicate for two basic reasons; they have a NEED to do so and they are REQUIRED to do so. This approach is probably closer to the mark for most businesses.

There is a relationship between people's own individual behaviour patterns and that expected of them by the companies they work for. The real question business owners need to ask themselves is whether their internal communication policies are correctly balanced so that both the psychological and the social factors that affects the way people behave, and therefore communicate, are sufficiently catered for.

The next question business owners need to ask themselves is whether they are providing the right psychological conditions within their business for team members to thrive and flourish. What are these conditions and how do you know if you are meeting them? You need to think about the following:

- Are your team members versatile in the roles they fill? Can they do more than one job?

- Are your team members involved in their jobs? Are they just going through the motions or really taking ownership of their jobs?

- How much time do they spend doing their work?

- How comfortable are your team members in performing their jobs?

- Are your team members skilled enough to carry out their tasks?

Get this right and you'll have a team that derives a great amount of job satisfaction from coming to work each day. Not only that but they'll ensure your business functions as efficiently and profitably as possible. You'll be creating an environment of trust that will ultimately allow you to spend less time working IN the business supervising others and more time working ON the business, planning future directions, strategies and growth.

Types Of Communication Models

There are horses for courses, as the old saying goes. The same applies to communicating in business. It should be apparent that there is no single communication model that should be used in any business. Businesses are all different; they have different cultures, functions and histories. They also operate in vastly different environments and require different management styles to survive. A company that is merging with another requires a completely different management style to one that is ticking along just nicely.

Generally speaking, most organisations fall into one of two broad categories; autocratic and democratic. They can also be categorised according to whether they focus primarily on work-oriented roles or people-oriented roles. Some could be a mixture of all four and would be thought of as being balanced.

Depending on what basic design the organisation has, a suitable communication strategy would be adopted to suit. Let's look at these in a little more detail.

Work-Oriented Organisation

A large factory would be classed as a work-oriented business. Here the communication style would focus on job-related matters far more than personal issues. Managers would be more interested in whether team members were meeting production quotas than on how they were doing in their social or family life. Relationships would tend to be more formal and structured and this would be reflected in the behaviour of team members at work. Internal communications would also reflect this.

Person-Oriented Organisations

A consulting business would be far more people-oriented than work-oriented and would place more emphasis on people than tasks. The overriding impression would be of a friendly, warm business where everyone gets along really well together. Now this might not be true; but it would be the impression an outsider got when dealing with the business. Internal communications would be far more personal and team members would be encouraged to have their say and be respected for it. People's needs are given a higher priority here than work.

Balanced Organisations

Family businesses are typical balanced organisations. Here family members intersperse family and business topics all the time.

Autocratic Organisations

The army is a good example of an autocratic organisation. They tend to be hierarchical in structure, with the different jobs being based on specialised functions.

Democratic Organisations

In these organisations, team members share their roles. They can be family businesses, small businesses or even larger progressive companies.

It's important to remember that, once you have determined which category your business falls into, you need to ensure your communication style suits. And remember too, that one communication style is not better than the others; they suit different situations. The important thing is to ensure you don't have a mismatch in your business.

Franchise Relationships – A Special Case

In the franchise industry, the question of relationships plays a very important, and prominent, role in the success of any franchise system. Relationships are vitally important.

These are some special considerations to bear in mind that don't apply to other types of business. You see, a franchise involves a very special type of relationship between the franchisor and the franchisee. This relationship is far more complicated than is the case with other businesses because it is a complex one, being both a business relationship and, at the same time, a legal one.

Apart from all the usual considerations that apply to internal and external relationships, you need to overlay them with the special considerations that apply to franchises. Pay attention to them and you'll be well on your way to running a successful franchise operation.

So, here then are those special considerations.

1. Keep your relationship with your franchisor (or franchisees) cordial. The nature of the franchise method of doing business means you will get close to your franchisor (or franchisees) and there is a very strong temptation to develop friendships. This is often the case the longer you are in business. Avoid this happening, as there will come times when disagreements will arise and you could have to resort to mediation. Also, friendships can become abused to get your wish across. "Oh come on John, don't worry about it. It is going to be just fine. Remember last year when sales were down and I missed two royalty payments in a row? I came good then, didn't I?" Taking advantage of a friendship is one of the most dangerous things you can do as a

business owner. Fallouts will be even nastier and more traumatic than if your relationship was on a more cordial and business-like footing. Recovery is far quicker after a business dispute and individuals tend not to get drawn into uncompromising situations. After all, business is business.

2. Don't procrastinate. Take decisions quickly and firmly. Remember, the buck really does stop with you. Avoid the temptation to flick any challenge to your franchisor (or to pass it down to your franchisees).

3. Business must be fun, so open up your communication channels. Work on balancing your business, private and spiritual lives. Don't let your business life dominate, as this is the quickest way to destroy the other two.

4. Try new things. Don't stagnate. The franchise business must be dynamic to survive. What works today might not work tomorrow. If you try something new and it produces fantastic results, let others in your system know. If you're a franchisee, pass this information on to your franchisor, who might want to incorporate it in the system for the benefit of others. If you are a franchisor, then actively try new things so your franchises can remain at the cutting edge of their industry. Constantly give them new ammunition and they'll love you forever.

5. Be willing to listen and learn. Don't think you have all the answers. Business is a two-way street and we all can learn new things every day if only we wanted to. Knowledge is, after all, one of your best weapons.

6. Abide by the system. Do what the system requires you, as a franchisee, to do. Remember that it has been tried and tested. And remember too, that business is very similar to baking; if you want to bake a chocolate cake, all you have to do is follow the recipe and you'll end up with the chocolate cake. But deviate or leave out a few ingredients and you'll end up with a very different result. Remember, when you buy a franchise, you are buying a system, so use it. Why buy otherwise? You'd be better off starting your own business from scratch if that were the case.

7. Learn to ask for help. Battling on just because you are too proud to ask for assistance will get you nowhere. All you may achieve (apart from failure) is the wrath of your franchisor.

8. Focus on your own success and not finding fault with your franchisor. That will get you nowhere and make you no friends. Don't become one of those noisy people who finds fault with everything. That's being a VICTIM and not a VICTOR. It's avoiding responsibility and blaming others for your own shortcomings. You will be falling into the trap of digging your own grave. You will become the victim of the self-fulfilling prophecy.

"One of the keys to success in franchising is to carefully select your franchisees."

Brad Sugars

▌ Conclusion

Now you have all the keys to enable you to successfully enter the wonderful world of franchising. Whether your interest is in becoming a franchisee, a franchisor or a seller of a franchise, you should know enough now to avoid many of the pitfalls others fall into.

You'll have a few other advantages too, like understanding the franchise industry and what makes it tick. You'll have a very good understanding too, of how the industry came about, its importance in today's global and local economy, and where it's heading.

But that's not all you will have gained from reading this book. You will have learnt first hand from me all about the mindset you'll need to succeed. You see, it's really all about attitude – you need to have the right attitude, or frame of mind, to win at this game. You need to understand the need to have fun while you're doing it and you need to understand all about relationships and human behaviour.

By having a closer look at what others have found, by hearing their stories as told by them, and by learning from my experiences, you'll not only dramatically improve your chances of succeeding in whatever you're doing in franchising, but you'll also be avoiding the trap of reinventing the wheel. Understand that business is just a game, and games have rules and a referee. Obey the rules and you'll not be sin-binned. Obey the rules and you'll get along with the referee. Break them and you'll have the ref watching you closely, whistle at the ready. Every player has to know and understand the rules of the game before they take to the field. They also have to develop a good working relationship with the ref and to respect any decision the ref takes.

Business in general, and franchising in particular, is just the same. Your franchise system is the game, you are the player and your franchisor is the referee. You could also be the ref, if you are a franchisor, of course. But you get my point.

Succeeding in franchising is as simple as that. Understand the rules and the importance of sticking to the rules and working on developing and maintaining a good relationship with those in your system, and you'll

Conclusion

immediately find yourself so far ahead of the pack it won't be funny. Then all you need to do is to play the game – or follow the system.

Now it's over to you. You have the keys; all you have to do is to decide whether to use them.

▮ Getting Into *Action* ...

So, when is the best time to start ?

NOW ... right now ... so let me give you a step-by-step method to get yourself onto the same success path many of my clients and the clients of my team at **Action** *International.*

Start testing and measuring now.

You'll want to ask each and every customer and prospect how they found out about you and your business. This will give you an idea of what's been working and what hasn't. You also want to concentrate on the five areas of the business chassis. Remember ...

1. Number of Leads from each campaign.

2. Conversion Rate from each and every campaign.

3. Number of Transactions on average per year per customer.

4. Average Dollar Sale from each campaign.

5. Your Margins on each product or service.

The Number of Leads is easy, just take a measure for four weeks, average it out and multiply by 50 working weeks of the year. Of course you'd ask each lead where they came from so you've got enough information to make advertising decisions.

The Conversion Rate is a little trickier, not because it's hard to measure, but because we want to know a few more details. You want to know what level of conversion you have from each and every type of marketing strategy you use. Remember that some customers won't buy right away so keep accurate records on each and every lead.

To find the Number of Transactions you'll need to go through your records. Hopefully you can find the transaction history of at least 50 of your past customers and then average out their yearly purchases.

The Average Dollar Sale is as simple as it sounds. The total dollars sold divided by the number of sales. The best information you can collect is the average from each marketing campaign you run, so that you know where the real profit is coming from.

And, of course, your margins. An Average Margin is good to know and measure, but to know the margins on everything you sell is the most powerful knowledge you can collect.

If you're having any challenges with your testing and measuring be sure to contact your nearest *Action* *International* Business Coach. They'll be able to help you through and show you the specialised documents to use.

If, by chance, you're thinking of racing ahead before you test and measure, remember this. It's impossible to improve a score when you don't know what the score is.

So, you've got your starting point. You know exactly what's going on in your business right now. In fact, you know more about not only what's happening right now, but also the factors that are going to create what will happen tomorrow.

The next step in your business growth is simple.

Let's decide what you want out of the business - in other words, your goals. Here are the main points I want you to plan for.

Firstly, how many hours do you want to work each week? How much money do you want to take out of the business each month? And, most importantly, when do you want to finish the business?

By 'finish' the business, I mean when it will be systematized enough so it can run without you having to be there. Remember this about business; a little bit of planning goes a long way, but to make a plan you have to have a destination.

Once again, if you're having difficulty, talk to an *Action* *International* Business Coach. They'll know exactly how to help you find what it is you really want out of both your business and your life.

Now the real work begins.

Remember, our goal is to get a 10% increase in each area over the next 12-months. Choose well, but I want to warn you of one thing; one thing I can literally guarantee.

8 out of 10 marketing campaigns you run WILL NOT WORK.

That's why when you choose to run, say, an advertising campaign in your local newspaper, you've got to run at least ten different ads. When you select a direct mail campaign, you should send out at least ten different letters to test, and so on.

Make sure you get at least five strategies under each heading and plan to run at least one, preferably two, at least each month for the next 12-months.

Don't work on just one of the five areas at a time; mix it up a little so you get the synergy of all five areas working together.

Now, this is the most important advice I can give you:

Learn how to make each and every strategy work. Don't just think you know what to do, go through my hints and tips, read more books, listen to as many tapes as you can, watch all the videos you can find, talk to the experts, and make sure you get the most advantage you can before you invest a whole lot of money.

The next 12-months are going to be a matter of doing the numbers, running the campaigns, testing headlines, testing offers, testing prices and, of course, measuring the results.

By the end of it you should have at least five new strategies in each of the five areas working together to produce a great result.

Once again I want to stress that this will work and this will make your business grow as long as YOU work it.

Is it simple? YES.

Is it easy? NO.

You'll have to work and work hard. If you can get the guidance of someone who's been there before you, then get it.

Whatever you do, start it now, start it today ... and most importantly, make the most of everyday. Your past does not equal your future; you decide your future right here and right now.

BE who you want to be, DO what you need to do, in order to HAVE what you want to have.

Positive THOUGHT without positive *Action* leaves you with positively NOTHING. I called my company *Action International*, not 'Theory International', or 'Yeah I read that book International' ... but, *Action International.*

So, take the first step ... and get into *Action.*

▐ ABOUT THE AUTHOR –

Bradley J Sugars

Brad is an entrepreneur for many reasons. By the time he was just 28 years of age he was the International Chairman of a global franchise that he started with NO capital. He had his first business at age 15, made a lot of money by the age of 22, lost it all by 22 $\frac{1}{2}$, then paid back all his debts and financially retired at 26.

At the age of 15, he employed his friends as paper delivery boys and gleaned a few dollars for the papers they delivered. Since then his businesses have become a little more sophisticated, yet still based on the same principle of finding something people want to buy then selling it to them, making sure he charged well, and gave great service.

By the time he'd finished University, Brad had completed a Bachelor of Business-Accounting and worked in 27 different jobs; from gardener to pipe maker, pizza cook to radio announcer, and disc-jockey to accounts clerk. One thing he'd definitely learnt; very few people ever really gave anything their best.

As soon as he'd left Uni he got a job selling and invested every single dollar he earned into training himself. Courses on money, investing, sales, business, personal growth - you name it, he did a course in it. He knew that to achieve what he wanted out of life wasn't going to be about how hard he worked, but about how much he knew. By the time he was 21, he was running four retail stores, had a photocopy management contract, and was earning a salary of $60,000 a year.

His mum almost had a heart attack when he told her that he had quit to go and work for himself. Being young and naive was probably a good thing. No capital, but a lot of smart ideas on how to create sales, how to market and how to lead a team of people. By the way, those retail stores increased profits by 39% in the nine months he was in charge.

He bought into a ladies fashion store, a 33% holding with no money down; just the ability to help them create sales. He increased sales by 93% over the first nine weeks and sold his interest back to the other partners just three months later. He did the same with a pizza manufacturing business; he took their product from just being sold into cafes and got it on the shelves of Woolworths, and almost every other small retailer in Queensland. He funded this growth with his earnings from the ladies wear store and was also doing some business consulting in his spare time.

It was this consulting that really led him to where he is today. One gentleman he offered his services to (he used to give away two hours of his time for free, just so people could understand what he could do for them) ran an international training company. This gentleman, Robert Kiyosaki, a best selling author, asked him to come and train his seminar promoters in the art of marketing. Little did he know then what was in store for him.

Training 30 seminar promoters in Hawaii meant that he was bound to go into the presenting business. Seminars in Hong Kong, New Zealand and in Melbourne meant the sale of the pizza business to create an international operation training and consulting to business owners and managers. Robert asked him to train at his Business School for Entrepreneurs in Hawaii later that year. That was July 1994, and 350 business owners from around the world, 11 trainers (mostly in their 40's and 50's) were there to learn from Brad. He found a business partner who could take care of the operations back home while he got out and presented seminars, did consulting and basically generated the cashflow. And that he certainly did with hundreds of seminars, as many plane flights all over Australia, New Zealand, Asia and into the United States resulting.

He arrived home in January 1995 to find not only was he was not only tired, sick of travel, and missing regular business, but he was also broke. Major business lesson number one; partnerships don't always work. What to him was VERY serious debt caused him to move back into his parents house, get a phone line connected, put a desk next to his bed and start all over again.

He almost went and got a job. And, eventhough he'd just spent the last 11-months teaching everyone else how to make money (and getting great results for them), Brad spent three full days just sitting quietly wondering why he couldn't seem to do the same for himself. At the time he thought that life could never get any worse.

Brad sent a letter to every one of his past clients, seminar attendees and everyone else he knew, offering his consulting services again. And, after a few solid days on the phone, he was back in business. He sat down and wrote out the Vision, Mission and Culture Statement of the new company he was going to create. He decided to stay in the business of training business owners, but this time he'd be sure to do it well.

In March of that year Brad's best friend from University began working with him. They worked from Brad's parents' 'granny flat'. Brad recorded sets of tapes while doing the seminars, kept selling and consulting during the day, and continued selling the tapes. They stayed back until about 10 or 11 each night planning and systemising.

It wasn't long before he'd paid back everything, saved a few dollars, and had a plan in place to create an amazing worldwide organisation. To cut a long story short, within three years and after many trials and tribulations, he managed to create a company called *Action International*. Employing 24 people in Australia, they took care of the business in Australia and New Zealand. A joint venture deal (worth several millions of dollars) was then signed to open an office in Singapore to service South East Asia and in 1998 he took the big decision to go global through franchising. 188,000 people had attended *Action* seminars by then, 14,300 had been through their intensive workshops, and 397 had benefited from *Action* consulting services.

Brad Sugars is currently the Managing Director and CEO of *Action International* Pty Ltd, as well as Chairman of the *Action* Group of Companies around the globe.

Brad is available for a limited number of speaking engagements each year. If you are interested in booking Brad as a keynote speaker for your next annual conference or business event, call *Action International* on +61 (7) 3368 2525. It's literally guaranteed that your attendees will say he's "the best speaker we've ever had," time and time again.

■ Recommended Reading List

Action International Book List

" The only difference between YOU now and YOU in 5 years time will be the people you meet and the books you read ..." Charlie 'tremendous' Jones

"And, the only difference between YOUR income now and YOUR income in 5 years time will be the people you meet, the books you read, the tapes you listen to, and then how YOU apply it all ..." Brad Sugars

- The E-Myth Revisited by Michael E. Gerber
- My Life in Advertising & Scientific Advertising by Claude Hopkins
- Tested Advertising Methods by John Caples
- Building the Happiness Centered Business by Dr. Paddi Lund
- Write Language by Paul Dunn & Alan Pease
- 7 Habits of Highly Effective People by Steven Covey
- First Things First by Steven Covey
- Awaken the Giant Within by Anthony Robbins
- Unlimited Power by Anthony Robbins
- The One Minute Salesperson by Spencer Johnson & Larry Wilson
- The One Minute Manager by Spencer Johnson & Kenneth Blanchard
- The Great Sales Book by Jack Collis
- Way of the Peaceful Warrior by Dan Millman
- Brad Sugars "Billionaire In Training" 3 hour Video
- Leverage - Board Game by Brad Sugars

*To order products from the recommended reading list call *Action International* on +61 (7) 3368 2525

∎ The 18 Most Asked Questions About Working With An *Action* International Business Coach.

And, 18 great reasons why you'll jump at the chance to get your business flying and make your dreams come true ...

1. So, who is *Action* *International?*

Action International is a business Coaching and Consulting company started in 1993 by entrepreneur and author Brad Sugars. With offices around the globe and business coaches from Singapore to Sydney to San Francisco, *Action* International has been set up with you ... the business owner in mind ...

Unlike traditional consulting firms *Action* is designed to give you both short-term assistance and long-term training through its affordable Mentoring approach. After 6-years teaching business owners how to succeed *Action's* more than 3,800 clients and 380,000 seminar attendees will attest to the power of the programs ...

Based on the sales, marketing and business management systems created by Brad Sugars, your *Action* Coach is trained to not only show you how to increase your business revenues and profits, but also how to develop the business so that you as the owner, work less and relax more.

Action International is a franchised company so your local *Action* Coach is a fellow business owner who's invested their own time, money and energy to make their business succeed. At *Action* ... your success truly does determine our success ...

2. And, why do I need a Business Coach?

Every great sports star, business person and superstar is surrounded by coaches and advisors.

And, as the world of business moves faster and gets more competitive ... it's difficult to keep up with both the changes in your industry and, the innovations in sales, marketing and management strategies as well. Having a business coach is no longer a luxury, it's become a necessity.

On top of all that it's impossible to get an objective answer from yourself. Don't get me wrong, you can survive in business without the help of a Coach, but it's almost impossible to thrive ...

A Coach CAN see the forest for the trees. A Coach will make you focus on the game. A Coach will make you run more laps than you feel like. A Coach will tell it like it is. A Coach will give you small pointers. A Coach will listen. A Coach will be your marketing manager, your sales director, your training co-ordinator, your partner, your confidant, your mentor, your best friend ... and, an *Action* Business Coach will help you make your dreams come true ...

3. Then, what's an Alignment Consultation?

Great Question? It's where an *Action* Coach starts with every business owner. You'll invest a minimum of $1,295 and during the initial 2 to 3-hours your Coach invests with you, they'll learn as much as they can about your business, your goals, your challenges, your sales, your marketing, your finances and so much more ...

All with 3 goals in mind ... To know exactly where your business is at now. To clarify your goals both in the business and personally. And thirdly, to get the crucial pieces of information they need to create your businesses *Action* Plan for the next 12-months.

Not a traditional business or marketing plan mind you, but a step-by-step plan of *Action* that you'll work through as you continue with the Mentor Program ...

4. So, what then is the Mentor Program?

Simply put, it's where your *Action* Coach will work with you for a full 12-months to make your goals a reality. From weekly coaching calls and goal setting sessions, to creating marketing pieces together, you will develop new sales strategies, and business systems so you can work less and learn all that you need to know about how to make your dreams come true ...

You'll invest between $995 and $10,000 a month and your Coach will dedicate a minimum of 5-hours a month to working with you on your sales, marketing, team building, business development and every step of the *Action* Plan you created from your Alignment Consultation.

Unlike most consultants, your *Action* Coach will do more than just show you what to do, they'll be with you when you need them most ... as each idea takes shape, as each campaign is put into place, as you need the little pointers on making it happen, when you need someone to talk to, when you're faced with challenges and, most importantly, when you're just not sure what to do next. Your Coach will be there every step of the way.

5. Why at least 12-months?

If you've been in business for more than a few weeks you've seen at least one or two so called 'quick fixes' ...

Most Consultants seem to think they can solve all your problems in a few hours or a few days ... at *Action* we believe that long-term success means not just scraping the surface and doing it for you. It means doing it with you, showing you how to do it, working alongside you and creating the success together.

Over the 12-months, you'll work on different areas of your business and month-by-month you'll not only see your goals become a reality, you'll gain both the confidence and the knowledge to make it happen again and again, even when your first 12-months of Coaching is over ...

6. How can you be sure this will work in my industry and in my business?

Very simple ... you see at *Action*, we're experts in the areas of sales, marketing, business development, business manage-ment and team building just to name a few... and, with 328 different profit-building strategies you'll soon see just how powerful these systems are ...

YOU, on the other hand, are the expert in your business and together we can apply the *Action* systems to make your business fly.

Add to this the fact that within the *Action* Team at least one of our Coaches has either worked with, managed, worked in or even owned a business that's the same or very similar to yours. Your *Action* Coach has the full resources of the entire *Action* team to call upon for every challenge you have. Imagine hundreds of experts ready to help you ...

7. Won't this just mean more work?

Of course when you set the plan with your *Action* Coach it'll all seem like a massive amount of work, but no-one ever said attaining your goals will be easy ...

In the first few months, it'll take some work to adjust, some work to get over the hump so to speak ... The further you are into the program the less and less work you'll have to do.

You will, however, be literally amazed at how focussed you'll be and how much you'll get done. With focus, an *Action* Coach and most importantly the *Action* Systems you'll be achieving a whole lot more with the same or even less work ...

8. How will I find the time?

Once again the first few months will be the toughest, not because of an extra amount of work, but because of the different work. In fact, your *Action* Coach will show you how to, on a day-to-day basis, get more work done with less effort.

In other words, after the first few months you'll find that you're not working more, just working differently. Then, depending on your goals from about month 6 onwards you'll start to see the results of all your work and if you choose to, you can start working less than ever before ... Just remember, it's about changing what you do with your time ... NOT putting in more time...

9. How much will I need to invest?

Nothing, if you look at it from the same perspective as we do. That's the difference between a cost and an investment. Everything you do with your *Action* Coach is a true investment in your future.

Not only will you create great results in your business but you'll end up with both an entrepreneurial education second to none, and the knowledge that you can repeat your successes over and over again.

As mentioned, you'll need to invest at least $1,295 up to $5,000 for the Alignment Consultation and Training Day, and then between $995 and $10,000 a month for the next 12-months of coaching.

Your Coach may also suggest several books, tapes and videos to assist in your training and yes ... they'll add to your investment as you go ... why? because having an *Action* Coach is just like having a marketing manager, a sales team leader, a trainer, a recruitment specialist and corporate consultant all for half the price of a secretary ...

10. Will it cost me extra to implement the strategies?

Once again, give your *Action* Coach just half an hour and they'll show you how to turn your marketing into an investment that yields sales and profits rather than just running up your expenses ...

In most cases we'll actually save you money when we find the areas that aren't working for you. But yes, I'm sure you'll need to spend some money to make some money.

Yet, when you follow our simple testing and measuring systems you'll never risk more than a few dollars on each campaign, and when we find the ones that work we make sure you keep profiting from them time and again ...

Remember, when you go the accounting way of saving costs you can only ever add a few percent to the bottom line ...

Following Brad Sugars' formula your *Action* Coach will show you that through sales, marketing and income growth your possible returns are exponential ...

The sky's the limit as they say ...

11. Are there any Guarantees?

To put it bluntly, no. Your *Action* Coach will never promise any specific results nor will they guarantee any of your goals will become a reality ...

You see, we're your coach ... you're still the player, and it's up to you to take the field. Your Coach will push you, cajole you, help you, be there for you and even do some things with you ... but you've still got to do the work ...

Only YOU can ever be truly accountable for your own success and at *Action* we know this to be a fact. We guarantee to give you the best service we can, to answer your questions promptly and with the best available information. And, last but not least your *Action* Coach is committed to making you successful whether you like it or not ...

That's right, once we've set the goals, and made the plan we'll do whatever it takes to make sure you reach for that goal and strive with all your might to achieve all that you desire ...

Of course we'll be sure to keep you as balanced in your life as we can. We'll make sure you never compromise either the long-term health and success of your company or yourself, and more importantly your personal set of values and what's important to you ...

12. What results have other business owners seen?

Anything from previously working 60-hours a week down to working just 10 ... right through to increases in revenues of 100's and even 1,000's of percent ... Results speak for themselves ... Be sure to keep reading for specific examples of real people, with real businesses ... getting real results.

There are 3 reasons why this will work for you in your business. Firstly, your *Action* Coach will help you get 100% focussed on your goals and the step-by-step processes to get you there. This focus alone is amazing in its effect on you and your business results.

Secondly, your coach will hold you accountable to get things done, not just for the day-to-day running of the business, but for the dynamic growth of the business ... You're investing in your success and we're going to get you there ...

Thirdly, your Coach is going to teach you one-on-one as many of *Action's* 328 profit building strategies as you need ... So, whether your goal is to be making more money, or working less hours ... or, both ... inside the next 12-months your goals can become a reality ... Just ask any of the thousands of existing *Action* clients ... or more specifically, check out the results of 19 of our most recent clients shown over the page in just a moment ...

13. What areas will you coach me in?

There are 5 main areas your *Action* Coach will work on with you ... of course how much of each depends upon you, your business and your goals ...

Sales ... The backbone of creating a super profitable business, and one area we'll help you get spectacular results in ...

Marketing & Advertising ... If you want to get a sale, you've got to get a prospect ... Over the next 12-months your *Action* Coach will teach you, Brad Sugars' amazingly simple streetwise marketing ... marketing that makes profits.

Team Building & Recruitment ... You'll never WISH for the right people again ... you'll have motivated and passionate team members when your Coach shows you how ...

Systems and Business Development ... Stop the business running you and start running your business ... Your Coach will show you the secrets to having the business work, even when you're not there ...

Customer Service ... How to deliver consistently, make it easy to buy and leave your customers feeling delighted with your service ... Both referrals and repeat business are centered in the strategies your Coach will teach you ...

14. Can you also train my people?

Yes ... in fact, we believe that training your people is almost as important as coaching you.

Your investment starts at $1,500 for your entire team and, you can decide between five very powerful in-house training programs. From *'Sales Made Simple'* for your face-to-face sales team to *'Phone Power'* for your entire teams telephone etiquette and sales ability. Then you can run the *'Raving Fans'* customer service training or the *'Total Team'* training ... And finally, if your too busy earning a living to make any real money - then you've just got to attend our *'Business Academy 101'*. It will make a huge impact on your finances, business, career, family and lifestyle. You'll be amazed at how much involvement and excitement comes out of your team with each training program.

15. Can you write ads, letters and marketing pieces for me ?

Yes ... your *Action* Coach can do it for you, they can train you to do it yourself or we can simply critique the marketing pieces you're using right now ...

If you want us to do it for you, our one time fee's start at just $1,195 ... and you'll not only get one piece, we'll design several pieces for you to take to the market and see which one performs the best. Then, if it's a critique you're after, just $349 means we'll work through your entire piece and give you feedback on what to change, how to change it and what else you should do ... Last but not least for between $15 and $795 we can recommend a variety of books, tapes and most importantly, Brad Sugars' *'Instant'* range of books that'll take you step-by-step through the how to's of creating your marketing pieces.

16. Why do you also recommend books, tapes and video's?

Basically, to save you time and money ... Take Brad Sugars' *Sales Rich* DVD or Video Series for instance ... In about 16 hours you'll learn more about business than you have in the last 12-years ... It'll also mean your *Action* Coach works with you on the high level implementation rather than the very basic teaching ...

It's a very powerful way for you to speed up the coaching process and get phenomenal rather than just great results ...

17. When is the best time to get started ?

Yesterday ... OK seriously ... right now, today, this minute, before you take another step, waste another dollar, lose another sale, work too many more hours, miss another family event, forget another special occasion ...

Far too many business people wait and see ... they think working harder will make it all better. Remember, what you know got you to where you are ... to get to where you want to go, you've got to mak some changes and most probably, learn something new ...

There's no time like the present to get started on your dreams and goals...

18. So, how do we get started ?

Well, firstly ... you'd better get back in touch with your *Action* Coach ... there's some very simple paperwork to sign and then you're on your way ...

You'll have to invest a few hours showing them everything about your business, together you'll get a plan created and then the work starts. Remember, it may seem like a big job at the start, but with a Coach, you're sharing the load and together you'll achieve great things.

Here's what others say about what happened after working wih an *Action* business coach ...

Paul and Rosemary Rose - Icontact Multimedia

"Our *Action* coach showed us several ways to help market our product. We went on to triple our client base and simultaneously tripled our profits in just seven months – it was unbelievable!Last year was our best Christmas ever – we were really able to spoil ourselves!"

S.Ford - Pride Kitchens

"In 6 months, I've gone from working over 60 hours per week in my business to under 20, and my conversion rates up from 19% to 62%. I've now got some life back!"

Gary and Leanne Paper - Galea Timber Products

"We achieved our goal for the 12 months within a 6 month period with a 100% increase in turnover and a good increase in margins. We have already recommended and will continue to recommend this program to others"

Russell, Kevin, John and Karen - Northern Lights Power and Distribution

"Our profit margin has increased from 8% to 21% in the last 8 months. *Action* coaching focussed us on what are our most profitable markets."

Ty Pedersen - De Vries Marketing Sydney

"After just three months of coaching, my sales team's conversion rate has grown from an average of below 12% to over 23% and our profits have climbed by more than 30%."

Hank Meerkerk and Hemi McGarvey - B.O.P School of Welding

"Last year we started off with a profit forecast, but as soon as we got *Action* involved we decided to double our forecast. We're already well over that forecast again by two-and-a-half times on turnover and profits are even higher. Now we run a really profitable business."

Stuart Birch - Education Personnel Limited

"One direct mail letter added $40 000 to my bottom line and working with *Action* has given me quality time to work on my business and spend time with my family."

Mark West - Wests Pumping and Irrigation

"In four months two simple strategies have increased our business more than 20%. We're so busy, we've had to delay expanding the business while we catch up!"

Michael Griffiths - Gym Owner

"I went from working 70 hours per week IN the business to just 25 hours with the rest of the time spent working ON the business."

Cheryl Standring - In Harmony Landscapes

"We tried our own direct mail and only got a 1% response, with *Action* our response rate increased to 20%... it's definitely worth every dollar we've invested."

Jason and Chris Houston - Empradoor Finishing

"After 11 months of working with *Action* we have increased our sales by 497%, and the team is working without us having to be there."

Michael Avery - Coomera Pet Motels

"I was sceptical at first, but I knew we needed major changes in our business. In 2 months, our extra profits were easily covering our investment and our predictions for the next 10 months are amazing."

Garry Norris - North Tax & Accounting

"As an accountant, my training enables me to help other business people make more money. It is therefore refreshing when someone else can help me do the same. I have a policy of only referring my clients to people who are professional, good at what they do and who have personally given me great service. *Action* fits all three of these criteria and I recommend *Action* to those of my business clients who want to grow and develop their businesses further."

Lisa Davis and Steve Groves - Mt Eden Motorcycles

"With *Action* we increased our database from 800 to 1200 in 3 months. We consistently get about 20 new qualified people on our database each week for less than $10 per week."

Christine Pryor - U-Name-It Embroidery

"Sales for August this year have increased 352%. We're now targeting a different market and we're a lot more confident about what we're doing"

Cheryl Standring - In Harmony Landscapes

"We tried our own direct mail and only got a 1% response, with *Action* our response rate increased to 20% ... it's definitely worth every dollar we've invested."

Joseph Saitta and Michelle Fisher - Banyule Electrics

"Working with *Action* our enquiry rate has doubled. In four months our business has changed so much our customers love us. It's a better place for people to work and our margins are widening."

Kevin and Alison Snook - Property Sales

"In the 12 months previous to working with *Action*, we had sold one home in our sub division. In the first eight months of working with *Action*, we sold six homes. The results speak for themselves."

Wayne Manson - Hospital Supplies

"When I first looked at the Mentoring Program it looked expensive, but from the inside looking out, its been the best money I have ever spent. Sales are up over $3000 per month since I started and the things I have learnt and expect to learn, will ensure that I will enjoy strong sustainable growth in the future."

∎ The 28 most asked questions about joining The World's #1 Business Coaching Team ... *Action International* ...

1. So, who is *Action* International ... ?

Action International emerged as an overnight success in 1993 when Brad Sugars began conducting seminars and workshops for the owners of small to medium sized businesses throughout Australia and New Zealand. For the first time ever, business owners had access to hundreds of amazingly powerful, yet relatively simple and affordable sales, marketing and team building strategies to transform their businesses, and their lives.

Since then, more than 380,000 people have attended *Action's* popular seminars, and more than 4,100 business owners across the globe have discovered that appointing an *Action* Business Coach was the best decision they ever made.

Action has been internationally franchised since 1997 and currently has hundreds of franchisees operating in 19 countries. It is also an active member of the International Franchise Association, and is currently rated by the US-based Entrepreneur Magazine as the 19th fastest growing and 123rd in the top 500 franchises in the world.

Driving the growth and development of the *Action* system is its charismatic founder and best-selling author, 32-year-old Australian Brad Sugars.

Integral to the continuing success of *Action* International is its Vision and 12 Points of Culture.

Action Team members across the globe are dedicated to pursuing our Vision of World Abundance through Business Re-education and abide by our 12 Points of Culture, which underpins everything we do.

1. Commitment ... I am committed to the Vision, Mission, Goals, Rules and SUCCESS of *Action International*, its current and future team, and its clients at all times ... I always recommend products and services of *Action International* prior to going outside the company ...

2. Ownership ... I am truly responsible for my actions and outcomes and own everything that takes place in my work and my life ...

3. Integrity ... I always speak the truth. What I promise is what I deliver. I only ever make agreements I am willing and intend to keep. I communicate any potential broken agreements at the first opportunity. I clear up all broken agreements immediately ...

4. Excellence ... Good enough isn't. I always deliver products of exceptional quality that add value to all involved for the long-term. I look for ways to do more with less and stay on a path of constant and never ending improvement and innovation ...

5. Communication ... I always speak positively of my fellow team members, my clients and *Action International* in both public and private. I speak with good purpose using empowering and positive conversation. I never use or listen to profanity, sarcasm or gossip. I acknowledge what is being said as true for the speaker at that moment. I take responsibility for responses to my communication. I greet and farewell people using their name. I always apologize for any upsets first. and then look for a solution. I only ever discuss concerns in private with the person involved ...

6. Success ... I focus my attention on the successful outcome of whatever I am doing. I have a willingness to win and allow others to win : Win/Win. At all times, I display pride, prosperity, competence and personal confidence ...

7. Education ... I am willing to learn from my mistakes. I strive to learn, grow and master so that I can help my fellow team members and clients learn, grow and master too. I act as an educator to allow my clients to make their own intelligent decisions about their future, remembering that it is their future. I impart practical, useable knowledge rather than just theory ...

8. Team Work ... I am willing to do whatever it takes to stay together and achieve team goals. I focus on co-operation and always come to a resolution, not a compromise. I am flexible in my work and able to change what I'm doing if it is not working. I ask for help when I need it and am compassionate to others who ask for help ...

9. Balance ... I have a balanced approach to life, remembering that my spiritual, social, physical and family aspects are just as important as my financial and intellectual aspects ...

10. Fun ... I view life as a journey to be enjoyed and appreciated and will help to create an atmosphere of fun and happiness so those around me enjoy it as well ...

11. Systems ... I always look to the system for a solution. If a problem arises I will look for a system correction before I look for a people correction. I look for a system solution in my innovations rather than a people solution. I follow the system exactly until a new system is introduced. I will suggest system improvements at the first opportunity ...

12. Consistency ... I am consistent in my actions so that my clients can feel comfortable in dealing with me at all times ...

2. What is Business Coaching ... ?

Since we pioneered Business Coaching through the 1990's, the term has become synonymous with performance and growth. But don't confuse it with Life and Executive Coaching – it is far broader than that. It's as focussed on the business, its team, its processes and its sales and marketing as it is on the business owner.

You see, the owners of small to medium sized businesses find it hard enough keeping pace with all the changes and innovations going on in today's modern world let alone to find the time to devote to sales, marketing, systems, planning and team management ... and then to run their business after that.

As an *Action* business coach you'll take your business experience, add it to our unique copyrighted systems, and together through weekly conversations, you'll coach these business owners to financial and personal success.

3. What do I do and what do I sell as an *Action* Coach ... ?

Your role as an *Action* Coach is to help the owners of small to medium sized businesses with their sales, marketing, management, team building, direction, goal setting and so much more ... Essentially you'll be their sounding board, confidant, mentor, coach and consultant. But you don't have to be a marketing guru to succeed ... The *Action* System has been designed to get results in a way that's both effective for the client and highly profitable for you.

As part of your arsenal of products and services, you'll deliver everything from Coaching Programs to seminars, and from books and tapes to video programs.

So as a Business Coach, what might your average week look like? You would probably spend it meeting with prospective clients, coaching clients over the phone, preparing and delivering seminars, conducting in-house training programs, critiquing your clients' marketing pieces, performing Alignment Consultations or selling the *Action* Planning Program.

4. Who should become a Business Coach ... ?

Only people with passion should become a Business Coach. That's because Business Coaching is a very passionate business.

So if you're passionate about business, life and love, then ask yourself this: Does the very thought of finding better and more efficient ways of improving a company's bottom line set your pulse racing? Are you the kind of person who is constantly striving to succeed? Do you always find yourself helping others? If this sounds like you, then read on ...

5. Why should I buy a franchise to become a Business Coach ... ?

You'll want an opportunity that provides you with a solid platform for entrep-reneurial freedom – and one that's based on years of experience, proven systems and ongoing training. You'll want to own a profitable and fulfilling business, yet you won't want to recreate the wheel. Only a proven franchise will provide all this.

6. Why should I buy an *Action International* Coaching Franchise ... ?

If you're going to invest in your own business, you'd better make sure it has every chance of success ... right? Why else would you want to go it alone, taking all the risks and facing an uncertain future? Smart people choose to go with the winners. Even smarter people choose franchises that not only give them every chance of surviving the first few years in business, but ones that maximise their chances of succeeding through having proven systems to support them every step along the way.

By choosing to buy an *Action* franchise, you'll be joining the World's Number 1 Business Coaching Team. Not only that, you'll become an integral member of the company that started the industry! You'll also have more than enough resources at your disposal to ensure your business buzzes from the word go.

That's right, you'll become one of hundreds of Business Coaches operating in 19 countries around the world. And they'll all be there to help and encourage you every step along the way. Now that's strength.

7. How much do I need to invest up front ... ?

Your initial outlay is approx. $88,000 inc. GST, and this includes everything you'll need to kick-start and run your business. Your investment includes a powerful and highly educational library of videos, audiotapes and books that will enable you to learn how to be successful in life, business and in your own *Action* franchise. It also includes a comprehensive 10-day live-in training program, which will teach you how to use the *Action* system and how to sell your services to clients.

Like all businesses however, you will also need to have additional funds in reserve (which you're prepared to use – if the need arises) as working capital for marketing, networking and other general office set-up expenses.

8. What do I get for my money ... ?

When you invest in the *Action* system, you purchase the franchise rights to operate an *Action International* Coaching Business. This provides you with the complete *Action* system that covers sales, marketing, and coaching. You'll also get your own personal success coach who will keep you on track, a global support group, and a network of other coaches with whom to share ideas, successes and experiences.

In short – you'll be getting proven turn-key systems that's taken more than 8 years to develop.

9. How much cash will I need ... ?

This depends largely on your own personal skills, expenses, needs and goals – and how big or quickly you'd like your business to grow. However, as a general rule, you should arrange to have access to working capital of between $10,000 and $20,000 to fund the initial cash flow requirements of your business, to set up your office and communications requirements, and to fund any travel expenses.

10. What kind of training do I receive ... ?

You'll be provided with all the tools, and knowledge, to have a dramatic impact on your clients' businesses – and to change your own life.

By the time you start coaching, you'll be a master of most powerful business secrets available. And you'll know the keys to multiplying business profits and generating wealth. You'll be fully equipped to achieve sensational results that will amaze your clients.

11. What level of on-going training do I get ... ?

Unlike a lot of other franchisee training programs, your initial 10-day training program is only the beginning of your journey. You see, you'll be stepping onto a continual learning curve, with books, seminars, workshops, conferences and internet-based chat groups and forums all part of the process. It's stimulating, and it works.

12. What level of support do I get ... ?

Action International has a two-tiered administration and support system, which provides franchisees with the best of both worlds. Your **Action** Group Office is responsible for the overall administration, direction, development and marketing of the network, while your Master Licensee will provide initial and ongoing support and guidance. This ensures that help is never far away.

13. So, how do I make money as an *Action* Coach ... ?

Your main income stream will be through Mentoring Clients, each of which will provide you with between $1,000 and $4,800 each month in revenues.

Seminars are just one of the lead generators you'll use to source clients, and considering you'll be consistently aiming for at least two Mentoring Clients from each seminar (plus those you convert from any of our other proven prospecting techniques) you'll find your earning potential will only be limited by your enthusiasm. One thing's for sure; you'll be pleasantly surprised at the end of each month.

But keep in mind you'll be running your business from a home office. This means your overheads will be far less than that of many other consulting businesses.

14. Do I need a Consulting or Coaching Background ... ?

No. However, a strong business back-ground is a must. If you have owned or managed a business before, or if you have a background in sales, then this is probably the business for you. However, you will need a sound understanding of business principles, plus an entrepreneurial spirit, the right attitude, and a healthy dose of motivation wouldn't go astray either! Be prepared to show us how much passion you have for helping others, and show us too, the amount of drive you have to succeed in this business.

15. Who will be my target clients ... ?

It's hard to think of a business that would not benefit in some way from *Action's* products and services.

Typically, however, our target businesses are those with annual revenues in excess of $150,000 (most average around $250,000) and employing between 5 and 50 people. Most of these business owners are Owner/Operators who are looking to introduce systems that can generate more growth or profit, provide them with more time, or produce better productivity from their team members.

We have found that most start-up businesses are either not financial enough to afford our coaching services or are still in the development and establishment phase of their business cycle. They do not normally fit our "ideal' business profile.

Similarly, many big businesses will have their own in-house marketing depart-ments working in conjunction with outside advertising and public relations houses, and therefore may not see a need for our services.

16. How will I get leads and sales ... ?

As you'd imagine, being a Business Coach you'd have all the latest lead generation and sales techniques available to you. You'll be using the full suite of the most powerful, tried-and-tested marketing tools available to develop your business. You'll also have access to the very latest thinking on the subject, and this will keep you ahead of the pack.

17. Why will business owners have me as a Coach and is there any real competition ...?

Everyone knows, and accepts, that sporting stars need coaches. Without them they simply wouldn't succeed. So what is it about business people? Why don't they, as a matter of course, have Business Coaches?

Well, times are changing. More and more of business owners realise that in today's fast-paced business environment, there's no way they can stay abreast of developments, let alone keep ahead of them. The case for a Business Coach has become unassailable. Well, to those serious about success, it has.

Furthermore, business owners find it all but impossible to receive objective answers from themselves. A Business Coach can see the forest for the trees. The Coach will make them focus harder on the job at hand, and will make them run more laps than they otherwise would. You see, a Coach will tell you what is going on in your business without getting emotional about it. A Coach will, in effect, be the Business Owner's marketing manager, sales director, training co-ordinator, partner and friend, all rolled into one.

You see, more and more business owners are discovering that, while they might survive without a Business Coach, it's all but impossible to thrive without one.

18. So who then is our competition?

We don't have any really – except all the other Business Coaching firms that have recognised the potential of what we are doing and are copying us. None, however, have anything like the tradition, reputation and resources available as we do.

19. Can I really get results with all types of clients ... ?

Absolutely! You see, the key to change in any business is its owner ... not you. The owner is the expert in the business, so by applying *Action's* systems, you can make almost any business fly. Add to this the fact that within the global *Action* team at least one of your fellow Coaches will have either worked with, worked in or even owned a business that's the same or very similar to that of your client, you'll begin to understand what I mean.

20. What are the keys to my success as a Coach ... ?

A successful *Action* Business coach is results-driven, motivated and willing to follow the system. Coaches who lead the field around the world not only run a highly profitable business and have exceptional client relationships; they also contribute to the growth and development of the franchise worldwide. Surveys show franchisees succeed because of an eagerness to learn and a desire to help others, a willingness to work long hours to get the momentum going, good people and relationship building skills, sales ability or a willingness to learn and apply sales systems, solid self-discipline and family support, an ability to take direction when needed and to read when necessary, having money in reserve and being willing to invest it, a willingness to take risks and to ask for help, and being well organized and a good planner.

Common reasons for failure include not following the system, not working hard enough or not doing enough marketing, going ahead despite family opposition, spending money on the good things in life before they had earned it, not enjoying selling to other business people, not having the self-discipline to cope with the responsibility of owning a small business, and being under-funded or misleading the franchisor on the amount of funds available.

21. Will this business work in my area ... ?

The funny thing about business is that it doesn't matter whether you sell paperclips or aeroplanes, one thing you can almost count on is that pretty much every business owner you talk to (wherever they live) will want more customers, more revenues and more profit ... the three things that they can't change – well not directly, anyway. And while every enterprise has a unique set of challenges, they all rely on customers, revenues and profits. And that's where your services will be in hot demand. So in a nutshell – yes, this system will work in your area, simply because most of the challenges Business Owners face are universal.

22. How many hours will I work ... and should I employ anyone ... ?

Like all new entrepreneurial ventures, the first 12-months will be the hardest, not because of the amount of work you'll do, but because the work will be different. The learning curve that our franchisees go through is steep – we can guarantee that you will learn more as an *Action* Coach in the first 12 to 18-months than you'll learn anywhere else. As a Trainee, you'll become a sponge soaking up information from every source – be it other Coaches, books, seminars or from personal experiences ... you'll want to know more about everything – which means you will be VERY busy.

Being new at the Coaching game, you'll be trying out all our different sales and marketing strategies, trying to find the strategies that will work for you in your business ...

So even though, initially you will be spending at least 25-hours per week marketing, selling and gaining knowledge, you'll find that as the business grows, you can divide your time more evenly between Marketing and Delivery. This should see you working between 40 to 60 hours a week in the first year of your apprenticeship.

We do recommend however, that when you have between 8 and 12 clients, you hire a Personal Assistant, or recruit an Associate Coach, so you can leverage your time more effectively. At this point you'll start to choose the hours of work that suit you, your clients and your prospects.

As you settle into your new business, you should be working around 2-hours per week per client with 1 hour spent coaching and the other doing behind the scenes preparation work.

23. Can I work at home ... ?

When you start up we recommend working from home with a separate space designated for your business. You need to be able to lock yourself away, and then lock up and switch off at night. When your business has grown, you may wish to take advantage of serviced offices or your own office suite.

A unique aspect of the *Action* business is that most of your client consultations are done over the phone. Therefore, you don't waste much of your valuable coaching time travelling to and from your client's place of business. This leaves you more time to work with your clients and to earn more income without eating into your family or leisure time.

24. What is my territory ... ?

It is the region in which you have bought your license and your regional Master Licensee will assist you in your local market. Most of your clients will be within 20 driving minutes of your office and most of your work with clients will be over the phone or via fax and email.

25. What are the on-going fees and royalties ... ?

Unlike most franchises, *Action* has a fixed $1,500 per month Royalty. No matter what you make, this fee is fixed for the term of your contract. 5% of gross revenues go to the *Action* marketing fund. Annual conventions and other training programs are compulsory and at your own expense.

26. What contracts do I have to sign ... ?

You will be required to sign a full legally binding Franchise Contract in line with local Franchise and Contract Laws. You will need to get both Legal and Accounting advice. You can go through the Full Disclosure Documentation with your advisors. Our obligations, the obligations of the Master Franchisee's and your obligations will be clearly laid out. It will be a minimum 5 Year Contract.

27. What is the term of the contract?

The usual term for a licence agreement is five years.

All licence agreements provide for renewal at the end of that term provided generally that the franchise has been conducted in accordance with the terms of the agreement during the previous five years.

Renewal may be for a further five years, and the terms and conditions of the new licence agreement will be as per those contained in the current pro-forma agreement.

28. Are there guarantees ... ?

To put it bluntly ... No. Your *Action* International Franchise is a business and as a result it is up to you to make it work. We will never promise any specific results, nor will we guarantee that any of your goals will become a reality. You see, just like you're the coach to your clients ... we're your coach and you're the player. It's up to you to take the field. We will push you, cajole you, help you, be there for you and even do some things with you ... but at the end of the day you still need to do the work ...

Only YOU can ever be truly accountable for your own success and at *Action* we know this to be a fact. We guarantee to give you the best service we can; to answer your questions promptly and with the best available information. We also promise to keep you up-to-date with new improvements and constantly keep striving to make your *Action* system better and more powerful. And we're committed to making you successful, whether you like it or not ...

How do I apply ... ?

We are just as diligent as you are in wanting to make sure the *Action* opportunity is the right fit for you. Showing your interest by learning more about us is the first step. The next is organising a one-on-one interview with your Master Franchisee who will ask you to complete an application form and a referee's page before starting your Due Diligence. Several meetings with other coaches follow this before an acceptance interview with *Action* Head Office, when your paperwork will be completed.

Congratulations, you have taken the first step ... Now on to the second ...

Millionaire In Training

90% of the stuff in this book is missing from most of the wealth creation manuals which are available on the market today ...

Designed to save aspiring Entrepreneurs a lot of mistakes, Billionaire In Training provides an essential framework for creating business success including strategies for increasing

AUD $34.95
(Incl. GST)

profit; a how-to guide for buying, selling and keeping businesses, how to keep yourself on track and moving toward your goals, the 5 Levels of an Entrepreneur and how to advance yourself to the upper levels.

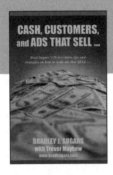

Cash, Customers and Ads That Sell ...

149 Hints, Tips and Strategies on writing Ads that Sell ...

Armed with all of Brad's super powerful advertising hints and tips, you'll be ready to write super profitable ads in no time at all ...

AUD $29.95
(Incl. GST)

With Cash, Customers and Ads that Sell, you'll quickly learn how to create profitable strategies and then how to create the ads that make the strategies work ... You'd be mad to pass up the opportunity to get this book.

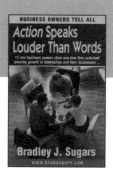

Action Speaks Louder Than Words

This book is about ordinary business people achieving astonishing results through business coaching. It chronicles the experiences of 17 businesses and outlines how they achieved phenomenal growth. You'll discover that the only real way to achieving amazing results for your business lies through business coaching. And you'll see it doesn't matter what type of business you run, how old or new your business is, how small or big, or even in what economy you're operating in, coaching can produce unimaginable results.

AUD $29.95
(Incl. GST)

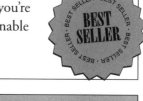

Leverage: The Game of Business

The rewards start flowing the moment you start playing ...

AUD $295.00
(Incl. GST)

Leverage is a educational breakthrough that'll have you quickly racking up the profits.

The principles you take from playing this game will set you up for a lifetime of business success. It'll alter your perception and open your mind to what's truly possible. Sit back and watch your profits soar.

$ales Rich DVD Series

Now you can learn the sales secrets that allowed Brad Sugars to financially retire at the age of 26. And, unlike most gurus, he started with NOTHING.

AUD $495.00
(Incl. GST)

Take advantage of the only multi-millionaire who will teach you exactly how he did it. In this six-video set, Brad gives you more than just theory; he gives you practical step-by-step instructions to take you from being just an average sales person to becoming a SALES SUPERSTAR. And all for just $495.

Millionaire In Training Video

Whether you've read the book or not, you've just got to view this video. Watch Brad Sugars in action as he fires up his audience, imparting powerful business secrets in an easy-to-understand fashion.

AUD $59.00
(Incl. GST)

Not only will you find this best-selling video great value at $59, you'll find it very informative and highly entertaining. It's no wonder he's widely regarded as one of the world's leading business speakers.

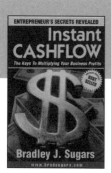

Instant Cashflow
(Revised Edition)

Now you can learn Brad's most amazingly powerful and user-friendly sales and marketing tips all in one book.

You will read this book once, then refer to it again and again! There are so many simple, easy and ready-to-use tips on how to boost your bottom line that you'll have to refer it to your family and friends as well. This new edition is now even more powerful because by working your way through it, you will be developing your own Instant Marketing Plan effortlessly and painlessly. It's a must for any business owner today.

AUD $29.95
(Incl. GST)

REVISED EDITION

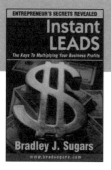

Instant Leads

One of the fundamental problems most businesses face is the generation of new leads. Without a constant supply of leads, they're faced with a never-ending battle to generate sufficient cashflow for the business to survive from one month to the next.

This book is designed to give you the inside track on everything you need to know about how to generate more leads for your business. It aims at providing you with an INSTANT guide on how to produce the various lead generation tools just like the professionals.

AUD $29.95
(Incl. GST)

BEST SELLER

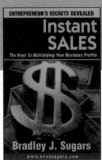

Instant Sales

By reading this book, you'll discover the secrets of selling. You'll also discover that the sales process actually starts well before you get to the stage of meeting your prospect face-to-face. You may even be surprised to discover this process actually starts with YOU.

AUD $29.95
(Incl. GST)

In this book, Brad Sugars explains how to maximise your Conversion Rate, or to put it another way, how to make sure your prospects actually buy from you. He also explains some not-so-well-known techniques that are aimed at smoothing your path through the sales process.

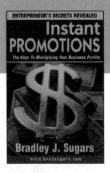

Instant Promotions

Brad Sugars knows a thing or two about promoting a business. Learn his secrets and follow his easy-to-understand and simple-to-implement steps to promotional success that will put your business on the map.

AUD $29.95
(Incl. GST)

This book is designed to give you the inside track on everything you need to know about promoting your business. It aims to provide you with an INSTANT guide on how to produce the various promotional items just like the professionals. Once you've read the book, you'll know precisely what it takes to successfully promote your business.

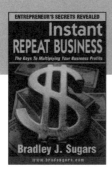

Instant Repeat Business

Hanging on to an existing customer is far easier, and much cheaper, than looking for new ones. Yet few business people realise this.

AUD $29.95
(Incl. GST)

This book is all about looking after repeat business. It's all about ensuring your existing client-base remains happy, loyal and content. It's all about ensuring you look after that 20% of your customer-base that accounts for 80% of your turnover. It's all about turning your existing customers into your most prized asset – Raving Fans.

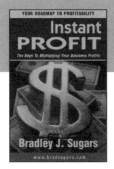

Instant Profit

One of the most common questions I get asked by business owners from all over the world is how they can improve their profits. You see, profit is the one thing they all want more of.

AUD $29.95
(Incl. GST)

And that's understandable, because PROFIT is the very thing they are all in business for. This book will teach you all you need to know about how to increase the profit your business makes. Think of it as a road map to profitability. Follow the general gist of the book or implement the strategies as they are; the choice is yours.

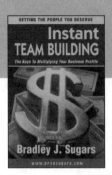

Instant Team Building

Do you know that a business is a reflection of its owner? Do you know that, as a business owner, you only get the people you deserve?

AUD $29.95
(Incl. GST)

This book is designed to give you the inside track on everything you need to know about how to transform your staff into a dream team and how to become a great leader. It aims at providing you with an INSTANT easy-to-follow guide on how to go about making sure the people you select are just perfect for your business.

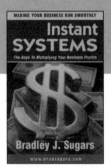

Instant Systems

This book is all about getting your business to work for you, rather than the other way round. It shows you all you need to know about how to work ON your business instead of IN it.

AUD $29.95
(Incl. GST)

This book is your step-by-step guide to systems and how to introduce them into your business. It will transform your business, freeing you up so you can devote time to other things like being with your family, starting another business or really looking for investment bargains in the real estate market.

Order all your Brad Sugars' products online ...

Getting hold of Brad Sugars' books and other products is now easier than ever before. Simply log on to bradsugars.com and buy online – it's as simple as that. Bookmark this site and keep up to date with the latest information from one of the world's leading business experts.

www.bradsugars.com

∎ *Action* Contact Details ...

Action International Australia

Ground Floor, *Action* House, 2 Mayneview Street, Milton QLD 4064

Ph: +61 (0) 7 3368 2525

Fax: +61 (0) 7 3368 2535

Free Call: 1800 670 335

Action International Asia

171 Tras Street, #08-177 Union Building, Singapore 079025

Ph: +65 (0) 6 221 0100

Fax: +65 (0) 6 221 0200

Action International Europe

3-5 Richmond Hill, Richmond, Surrey TW10 6RE

Ph: +44 (0) 208 948 5151

Fax: +44 (0) 208 948 4111

Action International North America

5670 Wynn Road Suite C, Las Vegas, Nevada 89118

Ph: +1 (702) 795 3188

Fax: +1 (702) 795 3183

Free Call: (888) 483 2828

Action Offices around the globe:

Australia | Canada | China | England | Hong Kong | India | Indonesia
Ireland | Malaysia | Mexico | New Zealand | Phillipines | Scotland | Singapore
USA | Wales

■ ATTENTION BUSINESS OWNERS ...
Increase Your Business Profits

Here's how you can have one of Brad's *Action* Business Coaches guide you to success ...

Like every successful sporting icon or team, a business needs a coach to help it achieve it full potential. In order to guarantee your business success you can have one of Brad's teams as your business coach. You will learn about how you can get amazing business results with the help of the team at *Action International.*

The business coaches are ready to take you and your business on a journey that will reward you for the rest of your life. You see, we believe *Action* speaks louder than words.

Complete & post this card to discover how the team at *Action* can help you increase your income today...

Action International ... **Business Trainers and Consultants ...**

Name . . . .

Position . . . .

Company . . . .

Address . . . .

. . . .

Phone . . . .

Fax . . . .

E-mail . . . .

Referred by . . . .